CW01656320

ABUNDANT BABY

The Abundant Baby Gentle Sleep Guide

Umbilical Cord Method: How to sleep from 7pm to 7 am

CHAPTER EIGHT
Publishing

First published by Chapter Eight Publishing 2024

First edition

This book was professionally typeset on Reedsy.
Find out more at reedsy.com

Contents

I

Introduction

If you're exhausted and can't keep your eyes open, save time by skipping to the back of the book where you will find:

- A summary of the whole book jammed into four pages
- FAQs from parents - look up your specific sleep problem and address it immediately
- Age appropriate sleep schedules

If you're still with me and awake, read on to find out how to teach your baby the skill of falling asleep independently so you can claim back your sleep! Twelve hours coming your way . . .

1

Mindset is Everything

Before we begin, I have one question. Are you ready?

Do not waste your precious time reading this book if you're not ready.

Introducing new sleep habits with a baby who is three months or older takes time, determination, patience and commitment.

To find out if you are 100% ready answer the questions below:

1. Are you exhausted?
2. Do you feel like something has to change?
3. Is your baby refusing to sleep for longer periods of time than forty minutes or refusing to go to sleep without constant assistance from you?
4. Do you think sleep is crucial for the brain development, happiness and health of your baby? (And yourself?!)
5. Are you willing to leave parties and social gatherings early so your baby can have an abnormally early bedtime?
6. Are you happy to become a sleep detective when looking

out for sleep signs that show your baby is ready for their next nap?

7. Are you ready for peaceful nap times and twelve hours of sleep coming soon for you and your family?

The good news is, if you answered yes to all seven questions, it's time to begin! You're ready and by committing to the process you'll be much more likely to succeed.

You can approach this sleep book with the confidence that I placed the upmost priority on the happiness of my precious babies and wanted to make sure they would cry for as little time as possible.

The aim was no crying at all, but the truth was, some tears did happen. The reality is that all babies cry and they will cry if you change their routine.

However, you are changing their current routine (where they probably already cry) for one that will ultimately result in no crying at all at nap and bedtime. It might take a few weeks to get there but you *will* get there. It is a happy routine where, as your baby gets older, they will feel in control.

The end goal is for happy sleep times and a happy baby and parent

With nobody crying! By believing this is possible, you will make it happen. When the going gets tough, don't change your new routine, stick to it, refer back to this book and video course at pages.abundantbaby.com for support and keep going.

Put aside at least two weeks now, clear a space in your diary, be prepared to give everything to your new sleep programme. Once you begin, this sleep routine will be with you forever and while it does give you excellent sleep, it also does require ongoing commitment. Twelve hours of sleep comes at a price!

If you're working and unable to put aside two weeks, speak to your babysitter or nursery and see if they'll support you on your sleep mission. You may be surprised just how helpful people can be.

And after reading this book, you'll be clear with what you have to do and be able to share your new sleep routine with your babysitter or nursery/pre-school.

With focus, determination and consistency you will get twelve hours of sleep for both you and your baby and your life will be transformed!

II

Ideal Sleep Routine

This book begins with the ideal sleep routine which is universal and suitable for your baby or toddler at any age

2

What Makes the Ideal Sleep Environment?

This book comes from the Abundant Baby Sleep course. I created this course with the sole aim of improving sleep for all babies and parents. If you prefer video content go to pages.abundantbaby.com to download a free mini course. The full course comes with detailed tutorials on age specific sleep obstacles like the six, eight and fourteen month sleep regressions, separation anxiety, teething and a refusal to nap. Everything you need for twelve hours sleep is there!

I have come across countless parents in baby groups and classes who are at breaking point. They see no light at the end of the sleep tunnel. They haven't slept for years and don't expect anything to change.

Believe me, it's normal to feel hopeless when faced with sleep deprivation because sleep is the vital component of your every waking moment as a human being.

If you haven't had a good night's sleep in a few months you'll feel sadder, hopeless, less motivated, more argumentative and less rational. Studies have shown that people with a lack of sleep, struggle to regulate their emotions and find it tougher to pay attention, process information and be more productive. There are countless mental and physical problems associated with sleep deprivation.

So, basically you can complain as much as you like! You have my sympathy. A lack of sleep isn't something you should get used to or learn to live with. It does not need to be a part of parenthood moving forwards.

You cannot live without sleep!

If you're currently sleep deprived and ready for a solution immediately, here's the best chapter first. I'm not holding back information. I don't want you to read a certain amount of this book and then receive the golden egg of sleep information as a reward. No, let's give out that amazing chapter now!

This is the routine to end all routines. Below, I will detail exactly how to create the perfect sleep environment. Without this your baby will not be able to sleep deeply or for a sustained amount of time.

Once you have finished reading this chapter, read the next chapter to create the perfect nap wind down routine. With these two components, you will be armed and ready for an excellent night's sleep!

So, what makes the ideal sleep environment?

The ideal sleep environment is dark, cool, silent and safe.

Dark

Use a black-out blind. Make sure every last bit of light is blocked out. There should be no night lights on in the bedroom and no lights flashing from anything electrical.

All electrical items should be turned off. You can keep the speaker for your baby's music (an essential part of the sleep routine) on, but cover it with a blanket so the light does not disturb the darkness of the room.

Cool

Keep the bedroom cool. The optimum temperature is between sixty five – seventy two degrees Fahrenheit or sixteen -twenty degrees Celsius.

Too warm a temperature can cause night time disruptions and a lighter sleep overall, so turn off the heating an hour before bedtime if necessary.

Silent

When your baby is younger they tend to sleep no matter what. But as they get older (than three months) they become distracted by anything and everything.

So, if you don't have a completely silent house (as most of us don't!) introduce music to create a constant, peaceful environment for your baby. This will block out any distracting noises.

The point of the music is to act as a sleep trigger to signify that it is now sleep time. It works well because you can take the music with you when you're on holiday or visiting family to create the exact same sleep environment no matter where you are. I use Brian Eno Apollo soundtrack. It works a charm!

Use a speaker which allows you to control it from outside the room because you'll be aiming not to enter once your baby is asleep.

It also means that after three or four hours when the house is quieter and you're going to bed too, you can turn the speaker off from outside the room without disturbing your baby, enabling them to enter a deeper phase of sleep without the music.

Safe

Make sure your baby's sleep environment is totally safe. This is the only way you'll feel happy to leave them to process and wind down before they fall asleep.

When a baby cries (at a level that does not concern you) this is often a way for them to process their day. It is imperative to leave them to it but you'll only be able to do this if you've made sure their environment is completely safe beforehand and your mind is at ease.

General safety rules

- Nothing in the cot – no bumpers, pillows, cushions or soft toys
- A cot with all four sides (not one retractable side)
- Use a baby sleeping bag, not a blanket
- Buy a new mattress that fits the cot
- Make sure there are no wires or anything that could fall or be grabbed
- Make sure you check official safety guidelines online before

being happy with the safety of your baby's sleep environment

Sometimes you'll need to go into the bedroom and check on your baby because you feel they're crying at a level you're not happy with.

Obviously, that's fine. You're the one who knows when it's OK for your baby to be left to process the day and when they need you. There's a difference in both cries and as you continue sleep guiding (not training!) you'll learn which is which.

Don't let your baby cry if you're not happy. Use your instinct and go in if they need you.

However, remember you're teaching your baby how to put themselves to sleep

You'll disturb the process if you keep going in too many times so instead monitor the situation from outside.

Try to wait for as long as possible before checking on them. Trust me, there'll come a day when you put your baby down to sleep and they'll fall asleep peacefully and easily with no crying whatsoever.

And let's be clear. That is not because you have made your baby cry it out alone. Your baby *should* be happy going to sleep.

You're teaching your baby how to fall asleep by themselves, not how to cry themselves to sleep. You'll simply get more tears at the beginning because they're not used to the new routine you're introducing.

Give the whole process time to work (at least two weeks). If you stick to the routine religiously, your baby will be grateful of the consistency and security that comes with that and you *will* reach a point of happy naps and bedtimes.

3

How to Get Your Baby Napping Like a Dream

When changing your old sleep routine, start with nap times because your baby will be less tired and they'll find it easier to respond positively.

Plus, when it comes to bedtime, they'll be familiar with their new routine because they'll already have practiced it at nap time.

The sleep routine you're introducing now will always be the same whether it is bedtime or nap time.

The only difference is, at nap time the routine should be shorter at around fifteen minutes and at bedtime it should be longer at thirty - forty five minutes.

Sleep Routine

1. Create the ideal sleep environment - dark, cool, silent and safe
2. Put a fresh nappy on your baby or toddler with a short sleeved t-shirt of muted non-stimulating colours. Take

their leggings, babygro or trousers off so there's no pressure on their bellies. They need to feel completely comfortable

3. If still breastfeeding or bottle feeding, feed your baby on your bed or chair away from their cot but still in the darkened relaxed environment you have created (**NOTE:** When your baby is a few months old it will feel impossible to feed without them falling asleep at the breast or bottle. While this is a challenge, the best way to do this is to pull away slightly to see if there's suction on the nipple or bottle. If there isn't, then they're starting to fall asleep. Stop feeding and move onto the next step)
4. Read a book (this is applicable from five or six months but feel free to do this earlier just for you. I know a lot of the baby books in our house are for me really because they're old classics that remind me of my childhood!)
5. Cuddle your baby standing up
6. Put your baby down in their cot. Pat them slowly and gently and say goodnight (**NOTE:** Just to be clear you are not sneaking out of the room. You are peacefully leaving the room, using the same words. Decide on a phrase and don't ever change it. For example, 'It's sleep time now. I love you.')

Going back into the bedroom

The aim is not to go back in. Feel free to wait outside the door to check if your baby is OK. If you absolutely have to go in because they are distressed then do!

However, if they're gargling or chatting or even complaining a bit, don't. Your baby is happy and should not be disturbed.

If they're crying at a heightened level wait thirty seconds before going in to comfort them.

I know this is painful but use a timer on your phone to make it easier. It will feel like an eternity but it is essential that you give your baby the chance to fall asleep by themselves.

They may surprise you and sound a lot calmer after thirty seconds or even stop crying altogether. If not, go in and comfort your baby (keeping the time in the room brief) and then say goodnight and leave again. This time wait outside for forty five seconds before going back in, then sixty seconds and so on.

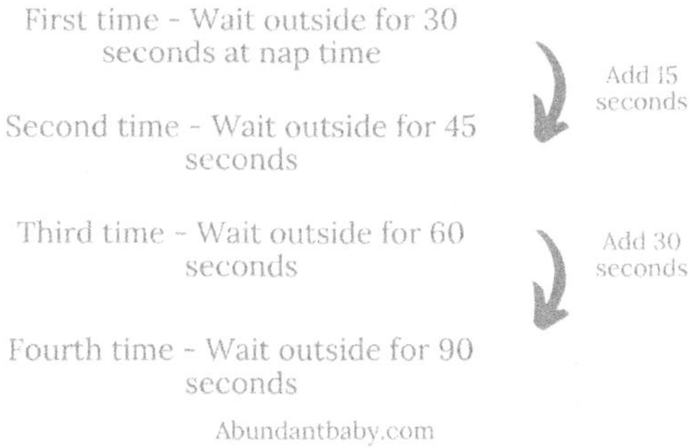

Go to pages.abundantbaby.com for a free taster of the full extended Abundant Baby Sleep video course which gives exact timings. Learn how to implement the above routine with absolute accuracy so your baby experiences minimal disruption and feels happy with their sleep programme. The aim is as little crying as possible and a happy nap and bedtime for the whole family.

Be brave

Know that you're doing the right thing. Wait outside as much as you can, rather than going in. Your baby needs time to process and to get used to this new routine.

Don't be scared of crying. It's natural to cry. As parents, we know when it's a cry that needs to be soothed and when it's a cry that's more of a casual complaint or a tired cry that will lessen as your baby drifts off to sleep.

When you know how to create a beautiful sleep routine and you know to leave your baby as much as possible so they can process their day alone, you've won.

By using your instincts and only going back into the room when you know your baby needs you, you're teaching them how to fall asleep independently and thus creating a fantastic and essential habit for life.

4

Why You Should Focus on Daytime Feeding

It's instinctual to want to feed your baby when they cry. They're pretty much always hungry so it's a safe bet to assume they need milk. It's also an excellent way to comfort and cuddle. Feeding acts as a moment of calm, as well as a point of nutrition.

However, you should have a different approach entirely at night time.

When your baby is over the newborn phase you should be slower to feed them at night. Don't jump up immediately. Instead (much like when crossing the road as a hedgehog):

1. Stop
2. Listen
3. Look

Stop

Hang on. Don't just spring out of bed, run over to your baby and immediately feed them like I used to (Ninja style).

No, instead lie still and take a minute. They might go back to sleep. Sometimes they're just calling out to check you're there. Don't presume they need to be fed straight away.

Listen

It's not about you laying there, feeling terrible as you listen to your baby crying and not going over because you're sleep training.

No, your baby might give a cry that sounds like it will turn into a full blown one but actually they could surprise you by turning over, getting comfy and going back to sleep.

If you'd not stopped for a second and listened, you would have already fed them and began a habit they didn't need.

Look

Check to see whether your baby is sad, hungry or whether they need reassurance. Pat or cuddle them. Don't presume they need milk every time.

Important Rule

From three months, at night time, feeding your baby is the last resort. Try everything else first. Of course, they'll still need feeding at night but it doesn't have to be the automatic go to every time.

Over the weeks, you'll naturally establish when your baby is genuinely hungry and when they're happy to go back to sleep with simply a pat or a cuddle.

After nine months, most, if not all, calories should be eaten throughout the day and should be super minimal (if at all) at night.

NOTE: The transition to less calories at night should be done gradually to ensure your baby is getting enough calories overall.

5

Circadian Rhythm

Waking up at the same time and going to bed at the same time everyday is important for the circadian rhythm.

The circadian rhythm is your baby's internal body clock which tells them when to sleep and when to be awake.

By waking up and sleeping at the same time every day your baby sets their body clock and lets their body know when to release melatonin (the sleep hormone) and when to stop producing it in the morning. This creates a better night's sleep.

Also, as your baby gets older they'll seek comfort in their sleep routine, so if their wake up and sleep time remains the same no matter what changes around them, they'll feel more confident and secure.

Although at newborn to three months old you are not establishing a routine yet, there is one thing you can do to help lay the foundation for an excellent night's sleep.

Let your baby know the difference between night and day

Keep talking to a minimum at night and avoiding putting any lights on. Only change a nappy if you need to. It's better to let your baby sleep than disturb them every hour or so to change a nappy.

If you need to change their nappy at night put a dimmed lamp on and make as little noise as possible. Don't interact or talk. Do the nappy change gently and efficiently so your baby can get back to sleep.

On the other hand, during the day, make sure there's lots of natural light in the house and go for a walk to reinforce the fact that it's day time.

Fresh air and exercise increase serotonin levels which will help to create a regulated sleep and wake up time so your baby finds it easier to fall asleep at the right times.

After three months

Look at the awake time and bedtime of your baby.

When your baby is first born it doesn't matter when they wake up and go to sleep, but now that they're three months old it's time to think about the circadian rhythm and work towards a seven a.m wake up and a seven p.m bedtime.

This is important for their quality of sleep and will make falling asleep at nap times and bedtimes much easier.

If your baby's wake up and bedtime is currently similar to yours (this is common and works well for newborn babies) you can adjust this gradually by making your baby's bedtime and wake up time fifteen minutes earlier every night.

Take your time with this change and don't rush the process. By making the change gradual you will keep disruption to your baby's routine to a minimum.

6

The Perfect Wind Down Routine

The perfect wind down routine involves sleep triggers to alert your baby to the fact that it is time to sleep. It prepares them for sleep and tells their body to release the sleep hormone, melatonin.

The nap wind down is a shortened version of this wind down routine and should only be ten - fifteen minutes. The bedtime version is the full extended wind down and should last from thirty - forty five minutes.

So, if you want your baby to be asleep by seven p.m you need to take your baby upstairs to begin their wind down at quarter past six.

During the wind down, take your time and drag out the routine for as long as possible.

You'll be surprised how challenging it is to make the routine last for a full thirty - forty five minutes. Reading a baby book doesn't take very long (after all, it only takes a few seconds to find out where Spot is hiding or to get to the page where Baby Bunting is safe and dry!)

Before the wind down begins, keep everything chilled and

quiet for half an hour. This will create a sleepy atmosphere and give your baby time to begin processing their day.

No screens, no sugar and no extremes

Extremes are extreme noises, exercise or stimulation. By avoiding any kind of extremes you avoid overstimulation and help to create a soothing mood.

Make sure play is relaxed, noise is kept to a minimum and baths are lukewarm.

Try and slow down too before bedtime as this will help. If you're settled and peaceful your baby will be too.

Wind Down Routine Schedule

6.15 p.m. - Wind down begins (Enter a dimmed, cool, safe bedroom, choose books to read and run the bath)

6.20 p.m. - Bath time (make sure it's not too warm)

6.30 p.m. - Read a book or two to your baby in their sleeping bag

6.35 p.m. - Feed your baby (or if they're no longer bottle or breastfeeding they can have a banana and a tiny bit of water – see below for approved bedtimes snacks that release tryptophan and help sleep)

6.45 p.m. - Brush their teeth

6.50 p.m. - Put your baby down to sleep in their cot. Whisper the chosen bedtime words to them which will always be the same. For example, 'Good night I love you. Sleep well.' Give them a pat, start the music at a gentle volume and leave the room.

Approved Tryptophan Bedtime Snacks

- Banana (this is the best bedtime snack. The below should only be chosen if bananas are not available)
- Oatcake
- Wholemeal rice cake

What happens if my baby cries during the wind down routine?

This is a good question and a worry for all parents. And the truth is, when I first began a sleep routine I didn't want my baby to cry at all.

In fact, this was why I avoided sleep training for so long. I felt incredibly sensitive to my baby's every emotion.

However, I quickly realised that *some* crying is inevitable because babies get used to the sleep habits you've shown them (even if you've created these habits by accident) and like everyone, they don't enjoy change.

Whatever routine you currently have that isn't working for you or your baby, it's still a habit and something which gives them security.

In the long-term, a gentle sleep progamme will be better for everyone but it doesn't mean your baby won't protest at first. After all, they have no idea that this is coming. They haven't read a baby book or decided it's time for new sleep habits. You have.

Plus, let's be honest, your baby is crying already, so why not create a sleep routine which will help them in the long run and reduce the amount of crying overall?

The end goal is to have no crying whatsoever at nap and bedtimes. This may feel like a long way off but it actually *will* happen! And often quicker than you think.

Some babies master their new routine in as little as a few days. Others take longer, around two - three weeks, but however long it takes, they will master it in the end and they will have excellent sleep habits for life, thanks to you!

I remember a friend commenting on how my second daughter (who was eighteen months at the time) always fell asleep so easily and peacefully at nap time and what a gentle nature she had.

I had to stop and think for a bit because while my daughter definitely has a gentle nature (as long as her sister isn't playing with her favourite toy!) I couldn't help remembering the determination it had taken me to introduce a sleep routine at three months.

There had been some moments I'd worried that excellent sleep and happy nap times wouldn't be possible but I'd told myself to think positively and keep going.

And here we are! It does take focus and determination but in the end it may look so easy that family and friends will assume it's down to genetics!

So, what do you do if you've followed the sleep routine perfectly but your baby cries as soon as you say the night time words and leave the room?

You're doing everything right but your baby isn't happy and

that's the last thing you want.

Here's the plan: The following steps will give your baby comfort because they'll know what to expect and they'll give you clarity because you'll have a clear set of rules to stick to.

The solution to crying

1. After your baby's wind down routine, leave the room and wait at the door to listen. Within thirty– sixty seconds your baby's cry may change to a happier, sometimes disgruntled noise, but often a gargle or chatter, that does not need comforting. This is when you've cracked it. You're teaching your baby to fall asleep by themselves. It's an important lesson to learn. They're processing their day and this needs to be done alone. Your baby needs to know how to calm themselves and how to put themselves to sleep. After all, they're the ones who'll be putting themselves to sleep when they're older. You can't be there when they're twenty!
2. If your baby is still massively upset after thirty seconds, then follow the timings mentioned at nap time. Enter the room briefly to soothe your baby - say the same comforting words and leave.
3. Try to avoid going back in. Only go back in if you need to. Wait for longer each time. For example, begin with thirty seconds and increase to forty five seconds and then sixty seconds.

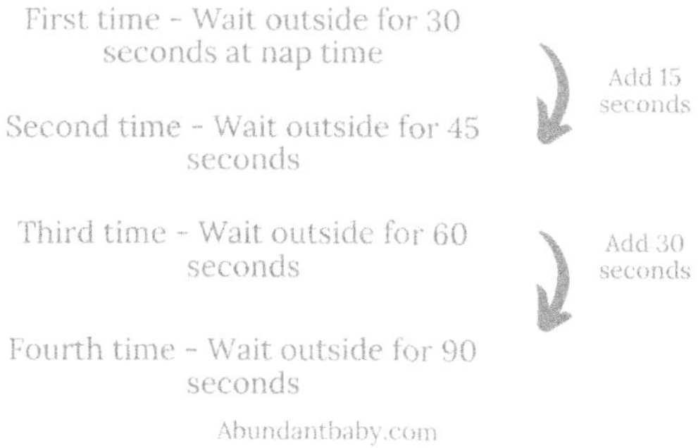

The idea is to create an environment where your baby isn't over-stimulated, they're relaxed, happy and comfortable. Everything's just right.

And do you know what the best part is? *You* can make all of this happen. You can create sleep habits that you'll be able to recreate anywhere, no matter where you are in the world.

You can create a sleep routine which your baby will even look forward to.

If you're on holiday or visiting family and friends in a new place, you'll be able to bring the sleep music with you, the black out blinds, the sleeping bag and the books and recreate the sleep routine exactly.

This routine will bring great comfort to your baby and an excellent quality of sleep no matter where they are.

It is something which lasts forever. It will always work. It may take time at the beginning to learn it and get used to it, especially if your baby has unknowingly acquired some habits that are not helping you or them, but give the process time. Don't deviate.

Once you have committed, you cannot change your mind.

Keep going. Keep it simple. You are doing the right thing. You're teaching your baby an invaluable skill for life.

III

0 - 3 Months

During the first three magical months of life together there should be no sleep routine at all. Read on to find out more.

7

Sleep and Feeding at the Beginning

First of all, congratulations! Your beautiful bundle of joy has arrived. At this stage no routine of any kind is needed. It's simply important that your baby sleeps as much as they want.

How much sleep does your baby need?

Newborn - one month old: Fifteen– seventeen hours of sleep (which consists of seven - nine hours at night and eight hours during the day).

One - three months old: Fourteen – sixteen hours of sleep (which consists of seven - nine hours at night and six -seven hours during the day).

When a baby is born they rely solely on you

They prioritise growing big and strong above all else. In order to do this they need to get the right amount of food (breast milk or formula) for growth and the right amount of sleep so they can convert energy from food into bone mass, muscle and tendons.

So, here's the kicker. . . At this early stage of your baby's life, you have a choice. If, like me, you love sleep and it's the most important thing in the world to you and sleep deprivation was one of your worries when having a baby, you can make a choice to prioritise it above everything else.

WARNING: This means sacrificing your social life and activities during the day in order to establish an airtight sleep schedule. However, you will be the one whose baby sleeps all night long and at every nap time without fail. Yes, that will be you! It's a commitment and it takes time but you will be rewarded.

Feeding affects sleep hugely

Feeding is a big part of sleep. As sleep and food are the two most important things for your baby, it makes sense that they go hand in hand.

Imagine you are the umbilical cord for your baby (unusual comparison I know but bear with me). In the womb your baby had food and sleep whenever they wanted. Now they're out on planet Earth and in your arms and suddenly they don't have food on tap anymore.

So, why not be the umbilical cord?

Give your baby milk (throughout the day!) whenever they want. This works well for breastfeeding as they cannot have too much. They know when they're full. It's totally fine to offer breast milk all day long to your newborn.

While this is slightly different with bottle feeding, it can still work. You will simply need to monitor the amount of milk your baby has more closely and make sure you keep to the recommended amounts of formula.

If you're able to always be with your baby, you can look out for hunger signals and feed them straight away, as and when they want.

Here's a list of hunger signs to watch out for to make sure you never miss an opportunity!

Remember, the more food your baby has during the day, the less they need at night (especially as they get older).

Signs of hunger

- Sucking
- Seeking
- Clenching fists
- Becoming irritable

Feeding your baby on tap throughout the day means that when it comes to night time you may feel happy to let them sleep longer at night.

This is totally down to you and the age of your baby as the recommended time to go without feeding at night between newborn and three months is no longer than three hours. Babies have small tummies and will need feeding often.

However, if you have fed your baby all day whenever they showed signs of hunger, you may feel happy to let them sleep for longer at night while still making sure they get all the food they need. This works particularly well with breastfeeding because they cannot have too much.

During the day when my daughters were in my arms asleep, I

used to feed them at the slightest irritability or discomfort.

If they didn't want any milk they'd simply go back to sleep or not suck. It was my way of letting them know that milk was constantly on offer if they wanted it. I believe it gave them the ability and peace of mind to sleep longer at night.

The first month was a blur

While the first month is a blur for us all, as the time goes on you should hopefully begin to adjust. And it *is* possible, even from the second month, to get more sleep than you perhaps may have expected.

For example, from two months old, both of my daughters would go to sleep at bedtime (at newborn - three months this will be your bedtime, so this was around ten at night), wake up after two hours for milk and then sleep for six hours from midnight to six in the morning.

I was effectively getting a normal (if slightly shorter) nights sleep of six consecutive hours and it totally transformed my life.

Example Pattern

10 p.m. - Feed and bedtime

12 midnight - Feed and sleep

6 a.m. - First feed of the day

Note: In the first three months there is no such thing as a sleep schedule so this is just an insight into the pattern my baby naturally fell into. You will fall into a different routine.

All you need to do is focus on feeding more throughout the day and of course be ready to feed at night, hopefully slightly less, but as and when your baby is hungry.

For me, at this age, leaving my baby to sleep for six hours was the absolute maximum that I was happy with and it took me a while to feel comfortable with this.

Any longer than six hours is not a good idea at this age and a lot of mothers would think longer than three hours is not good so don't do anything you're not happy with.

It felt right for me but it won't feel right for a lot of parents. And it is not recommended by health practitioners!

Throughout your baby's life the priority is, of course, excellent sleep but it's also about finding what is best for you and your baby so always go with your heart. It's your call. Take advice but trust your intuition.

8

Four Rules to Follow in The Early Months

There are four rules which will create a strong foundation of excellent sleep at the newborn to three month stage. These rules will help you to establish a sleep routine more easily when your baby is older and ready for one.

Introduce a clear difference between night and day

CASE STUDY: My friend, stayed on the sofa all day and night feeding and cuddling her newborn baby. She was exhausted and probably in shock after giving birth. Plus, it seemed liked her baby was happiest when in her arms and nowhere else.

Of course, she would go out occasionally during the day but not as much as she used to do and she would often not get into bed at night. Instead, she would stay on the sofa with her baby.

When her baby turned three months old he stopped sleeping at night. He would happily sleep during the day but it was as if he was ready to play at night time. He would not sleep at all. In fact, he slept for longer stretches during the day.

My friend felt hopeless. She had no clue what to do.

SOLUTION: This is an excellent example of night and day getting mixed up. Because there was no obvious difference between night and day my friend's baby had no idea when he was supposed to be sleeping and when he wasn't.

Establishing a clear difference between night and day will stop a situation like this from happening and help both you and your baby with your physical and mental health.

Everyone needs to rest after childbirth and it's important to go slow if you can and take your time with recovery.

So, don't rush this first rule. Whenever you feel able to and only when you feel ready, go for a gentle walk with your baby.

Don't worry about disturbing your baby if they're asleep

Get them ready for their walk and in their pram, whether they're asleep or not. Babies sleep so much at this stage. If they're tired they'll sleep regardless of where you are. You don't have to stay in the house or be extra careful around them.

Go to a café and enjoy getting out in the world and people watching.

This felt like such a big deal for me with my first born. I'd get nervous at the thought of getting myself and my baby ready and being out in the world, in case I had to change a nappy or breastfeed in public but as soon as I was out it would change my day and make me feel so much better.

That's the beauty of this rule, it has the added bonus of improving your mental health and confidence by adding variety to your day and giving you a change of scenery.

You can continue to establish a clear difference between night and day when you get back home by not being quiet. Do everything you would normally do.

Don't tiptoe around the house

If your house is naturally quiet, that's fine but make sure you're getting out for a daily walk with your baby and doing everything you normally would during the day, like hoovering or banging about in the kitchen.

This rule can go against your instinct as a parent as you naturally feel compelled to be quiet while your baby is sleeping but the truth is, they'll sleep through everything and anything. It's more important that they begin to know the difference between night and day.

So, as a contrast, when it comes to night time, keep everything quiet and dark. Don't change your baby's nappy as often. In fact, I like to leave the nappy completely.

Of course, a nappy must be changed sometimes but do this in dimmed lighting with no talking. It's sleep time. Not play time.

You are your baby's only indication of night and day so keep everything quiet and dark at night time to let your baby know it is time to sleep.

Encourage thumb sucking

Thumb sucking is an absolute life saver. Dummies don't work for uninterrupted sleep because they can fall out, which will mean your baby will wake up and rely on you to pick up the dummy and give it back to them. Hence your sleep has been interrupted.

However, a thumb is always there to comfort them. There's no way they're going to lose it! It's honestly the most amazing thing ever and it's actually a very natural thing to do.

It's one of the first things your baby learns to do in the womb. Babies start sucking their thumbs as early as the tenth week when they're the size of strawberry. How cute is that?

With my first born, she would start sucking her thumb during the night and make loud noises so I'd sprint over thinking she needed me. I'd immediately replace her thumb with my nipple thinking I was doing a wonderful thing.

However, with hindsight I now know she was trying to comfort herself and I should have let her do that.

With my second born I didn't immediately dash over! I let her suck her thumb and waited for her to call out for me, rather than preempting this and offering milk when she didn't need it.

Become the umbilical cord

As mentioned in the previous chapter, this is your role during the day and will be for several months. While there shouldn't be any routine in the first three months, even at this early stage you can still aim to feed all day and less during the night.

Do this by being slower to respond at night. For example, if your baby stirs, take your time and don't rush over to help. Stop, Look, Listen. Are they hungry or are they simply settling themselves back to sleep?

In all honesty, this applies more to your baby as they get older. For now, in the first few months, your baby *is* usually hungry. They will need to eat often and will wake up to do this.

However, Stop, Look and Listen is still worth doing now as it gets you into a good habit. Just remember that in the newborn phase this is a brief check and will usually result in you feeding your baby.

Your newborn baby needs as much milk and sleep during the day and night as they can get in their first few months. They have smaller tummies and will need feeding more frequently.

This is why most parents will wake a baby at night to feed them to make sure they're getting enough sustenance.

It's your choice if you decide they've had loads of milk during the day and you're happy to let them sleep for longer than three hours.

Perhaps start with four hours - wake them up and feed them. And then try five hours. If you're happy and they're feeding lots during the day then you can increase to six hours only if you're happy and only near the end of the age bracket when your baby is closer to three months old.

Avoid overstimulation

In the first few weeks, your baby will fall asleep anywhere and everywhere. However, as they get closer to three months, you may start seeing signs of overstimulation.

It's easy for your baby to become overstimulated as they notice more and more of what's going on around them. Your baby is constantly observing and learning new things.

For you a situation or environment may seem peaceful or relaxed but for your baby it is SO busy!

They're looking at the way the light creates patterns on the wall, the contrast between a shape on the rug or the way the curtains flutter next to an open window.

The world is new to your baby and they notice everything so

it's easy for them to become overstimulated.

After all, they *have* spent the majority of their life so far in the peace and darkness of the womb.

Overstimulation is a big thing to watch out for because it can lead to the release of the stress hormone, cortisol, which will stop your baby from sleeping and lead to overtiredness.

Here's what to do if you see signs of overstimulation

- Restless
- Seeking more comfort than normal
- Making jerky movements

Remove your baby from their current situation into a soothing environment (dark, cool, silent and safe).

Let's be clear, you're not aiming to make your baby sleep in this situation. Instead, you're simply giving them a moment to process and rest from the stimulation they were experiencing.

Overstimulation can happen so easily - just a change of scenery can be enough to overload your baby.

For example, when we took my daughter to her great granny's house for the first time the decor was totally different to ours.

Our daughter went from minimal furniture and grey and cream at home to orange and yellow and red all around her with busy patterned wallpaper, lamps and ornaments (my gran loves an ornament!)

It was too much. Her eyes were darting around the room. There was so much to see. Sometimes there isn't a lot you can do, aside from beginning a full renovation!

However, we attempted to calm the room down as much as possible by tidying, clearing and removing any ornaments or decorations that were easy to put back afterwards.

This may seem rude but my family didn't mind. Plus, if you do everything as carefully as possible like popping things into drawers or cupboards, you can easily move things back when you leave.

This will cause as little offense as possible while allowing your baby to rest their eyes and calm down.

It's important for you and your baby to be in new environments and not shy away from experiencing life but it's equally essential that you recognise the likely risk of overstimulation.

NOTE: If you want to keep stimulation to an absolute minimum during the first three months of your baby's life, don't have any screens and choose minimal toys.

Obviously, as parents, it's fun to indulge and buy gorgeous things for your baby so this can feel like a challenging rule but at this age your baby is so stimulated already by all the new things they're seeing and learning in normal life that they surprisingly do not need many toys and *definitely* do not need screens.

If you can't resist the gorgeous toys (I know I couldn't) choose natural colours and materials as much as possible. Too bright and too loud will simply be too much for your baby at this age and impair sleep.

The truth is, for the first three months of your baby's life, all they need is you!

Summary of the four rules

1. Introduce a clear difference between day and night
2. Encourage thumb sucking
3. Become the umbilical cord

4. Avoid overstimulation

IV

3 - 6 Months

Welcome to the next three months! Things can get tricky here as you deal with your first major sleep regression. Read on to find out what to do.

9

How to Cope With the Four Month Sleep Regression

Sleep regressions can be intense and challenging (understatement of the year!)

However, a sleep regression is a sign you're doing everything right because your baby is developing and progressing as they should.

In fact, instead of a regression I like to say a development because a sleep regression is a sign your baby's brain has reached it's next phase of development.

Now, let's talk about how to cope with this change and how to stop it from ruining your excellent work on sleep so far.

Your baby's brain is advancing from the newborn sleep they experienced at zero to three months, where they could sleep anywhere and everywhere, to something that looks more like adult sleep.

Babies will now begin producing melatonin, which means they sleep in cycles like an adult does and will wake briefly between cycles.

In order for your baby to go back to sleep when they wake up, their environment has to be exactly the same as the one they fell asleep in.

They can no longer fall asleep in your arms and be put down in their cot because this is a different place and it will totally disarm them.

Imagine how you would feel if you fell asleep in your bed and woke up on the roof!

So, how can you help your baby?

And how can you help yourself?

You might be finding this sleep regression tough.

I know I was with my first daughter. At around three months it was a challenging time.

When my daughter was newborn she used to fall asleep everywhere and anywhere - in my arms at home or out and about in her pram in cafes. It didn't matter. Even the loudest coffee machines in the world wouldn't wake her up.

I was in awe. I'd never had a baby before so I thought what's the big fuss? The sleep part is the easy part.

How wrong I was!! At three months old . . . everything changed. Suddenly my daughter wouldn't fall asleep anywhere. She began resisting sleep and even crying when I offered her milk (she would usually fall asleep while feeding).

I had no idea that three months is an essential time to introduce sleep guidance because of the huge change your baby's brain is going through.

So, if your baby has suddenly stopped sleeping, this chapter is for you!

Case study

My first born would always fall asleep in my arms after breast-feeding. It was a peaceful time for both of us and it was a total guarantee. Feed my baby and she would fall asleep.

However, at around three months, she started crying when I offered to feed her. She would resist and turn away. I knew she was hungry so I couldn't work out what the problem was.

I was scared my baby didn't like my milk anymore, that it had somehow changed flavour or that she wasn't feeling happy for a reason unknown to me.

She was getting more and more tired and agitated. I'd pace up and down the living room totally at a loss. Why was my peaceful baby who loved to eat and sleep suddenly resisting everything?

Here's the problem

The thought of breastfeeding made my baby feel anxious because she was falling asleep while drinking milk in my arms and waking up somewhere else.

I would put her down in her cot as soon as she fell asleep in my arms. It meant I knew she was safe and I could do other jobs or relax while she slept.

However, it wasn't good for her. She was expecting to wake up in my arms and was waking up somewhere completely different.

She didn't want to breastfeed because she'd worked out that that was the trigger to falling asleep and waking up in a different place. So she cried to avoid it and absolutely refused to sleep.

Here's the solution

The solution is (at three months of age or older) have a clear place for your baby to sleep during the day. The best choice is in their cot where they sleep at night.

You will now become the guardian of your baby's sleep. As soon as your baby turns three months old, every waking moment will be spent observing them and spotting sleep signals.

You'll monitor how long they're awake for and how long they sleep for. As soon as they're ready to sleep you will take them to their cot away from the distractions of the house and begin the wind down (go to chapter six for a reminder or get a free taster of the full extended Abundant Baby Sleep course at pages.abundantbaby.com).

At this age your baby will only be able to stay awake for forty five to sixty minutes.

Some babies can be awake for as long as two hours at a time, which is perfectly fine as long as they're happy and not displaying sleep signals.

The total sleep needed at three to four months is fourteen and a half hours. This should be between three and a half hours to four and half during the day and between ten to eleven hours at night.

Total sleep needed between 3 - 4 months: 14.5 hours

- **Day time:** 3.5 - 4.5 hours
- **Night time:** 10 - 11 hours

NOTE: Timings are only given as a guidance. The most important thing at every stage is whether your baby is sleepy or not.

All babies are different so while they will need similar amounts of sleep, it won't be exactly the same. Sleep signals govern whether you put your baby down for a nap at this stage not example sleep schedules.

What are sleep signals?

Sleep signals are your baby's way of telling you that they're tired. Each baby will have slightly different ones and you will learn to recognise them easily.

At first, it may seem overwhelming or challenging to spot the signs but don't worry.

If in doubt, trust your instinct and take your baby up to bed. It will get easier to spot the signs, the more you do it. Trust me.

Five most common sleep signals

1. Avoiding eye contact/ staring into the distance
2. Rubbing eyes or ears
3. Red eyes
4. Jerky movements
5. Becoming fussy/ wanting to nurse or cuddle more often

These are the most common signs. All babies will show at least a few of the above list and perhaps a few of their own, which you will become used to in time.

I haven't included the most obvious sign which is one you would normally associate with sleep – yawning. This is because yawning is one step too far.

Yawning means your baby is getting dangerously close to being over-tired and will be more challenging to put to sleep. It is your last chance.

You don't want to see your baby yawning. It's too late at that point. You have missed the ideal window to put your baby down to sleep.

To catch the ideal sleep window, take your baby up to sleep immediately as soon as you notice any of the above signs. It doesn't matter if they've only been awake for thirty minutes. Just do it.

Don't overthink it

If your baby is tired they should nap. At this early stage, the most important thing your baby can do is sleep.

You're nourishing your baby with food, now you must nourish them with sleep too.

Summary

Between three to six months all you should be thinking about is sleep. You will be constantly watching your baby, ready to detect any sleep signals so you can whisk them off to bed for their next nap.

You may end up having a baby who naps four or five times a day and that's absolutely fine. Both my daughters even occasionally had six naps at this age depending on the day and their level of tiredness.

Don't hold back sleep for your baby throughout the day at this age. It will not work. You will simply get an overtired baby who will not nap during the day or sleep at night.

Sleep promotes sleep. Naps will do no harm to night time sleeping.

ALL HAIL SLEEP!

10

Sleep Crutches

A baby who can fall asleep by themselves is a baby who will sleep through the night when it is healthy and safe to do so because they have the skills to make it possible.

Especially after the four month regression, teaching the skill of falling asleep independently is crucial because it means when your baby wakes up throughout the night (as we all do multiple times) they will be able to get themselves back to sleep without disturbing you.

This is the reason an older baby may *still* not sleep through the night. They have learned to call out for you, instead of soothing themselves back to sleep.

At three to four months it can take a couple of weeks to teach a baby to fall asleep by themselves. However, some may take as little as few days.

One thing's for sure, no matter how long or short your baby takes to adjust, consistency will get you there.

By ensuring you have created an ideal sleep environment and by always sticking to your wind down routine (as mentioned in chapter six and the Abundant Baby Sleep Course) you will get there. Do not waver or change the routine.

One crucial thing needed is a total lack of sleep crutches.

Sleep crutches are things that your baby relies on to get to sleep but are out of your control so you cannot re-introduce them to help your baby get back to sleep without disturbing your own sleep.

Four common sleep crutches

- A dummy/soother
- Feeding to sleep
- Rocking/patting to sleep
- Holding or cuddling to sleep

The thing about a sleep crutch is, if a baby has gone to sleep breastfeeding or being patted on the back, when they wake up they will immediately search for the exact situation they fell asleep in.

Whether this is the hand that was patting them, the dummy, bottle or nipple they were sucking, or the arms that were cuddling them, they will wonder where they have gone and will cry to get them back.

This is why sleep crutches do not work as a long term way to get your baby to fall asleep. I know they work amazingly at the time but they do not work when your baby wakes up in the night. You need sleep too!

The solution is a sleep trigger. Replace all sleep crutches with a sleep trigger.

What is a sleep trigger?

A sleep trigger is the remedy for a sleep crutch. It is the direct replacement. A sleep trigger, like a sleep crutch, is something your baby becomes reliant on to go to sleep.

However, a sleep trigger is within your control. You have chosen it, so it aids your sleep rather than disrupts your sleep.

Sleep triggers

- A sleeping bag
- Lullaby music (Try the Brian Eno Apollo album)
- Darkness
- Sucking their thumb

If your baby fell asleep by themselves in their cot wrapped up in their sleeping bag, sucking their thumb and listening to music, when they wake up briefly during the night or even during a long nap, they will see their surroundings are the same and go back to sleep.

If they don't go back to sleep because the environment has changed (perhaps you turned the music off for a deeper sleep) then you can put it back on via a remote control.

This is why a Bluetooth speaker is essential because it means you do not need to enter the room in which your baby is sleeping and they will go back to sleep without any kind of disturbance. They will be soothed.

During a nap, it's fine to keep the music on for the whole time especially as your house is likely to be busier and louder.

At night, however, it's important to turn the music off after a few hours, when everyone else goes to bed, as this enables your baby to enter a deeper sleep.

The point is, with sleep triggers you are in control but with sleep crutches you're not.

Sleep crutches are created when you're trying your best to help your baby sleep and you desperately find a way to do that but later that way becomes a hindrance because your baby needs it to go back to sleep and you can't give it to them without disrupting your own sleep.

Understanding sleep windows

A sleep window is a period of ten to fifteen minutes when your baby will find it easy to fall asleep. During this window your baby is the perfect amount of tired: ready to sleep but not overtired.

You can achieve this blissful state by watching out for your baby's sleep signals and taking them for a nap as soon as you see, for example, rubbing of the eyes or staring into space.

When you understand sleep windows and how long your baby should be awake for between naps, you can completely avoid crying.

There's a sweet spot when your baby will be placed down in the cot, drowsy but *not* asleep and have time to process the last forty five minutes of being awake.

This is completely possible. It may sound like a dream but it *is* possible. If I can do it, you can do it.

I achieved cry free nap and bedtimes with both my daughters and you can most certainly do it with your babies too.

It took me ages with my first daughter because I didn't know what I was doing but it was much easier the second time around because all I had to do was put the sleep routine into practice.

Sure, it does take a lot of focus

You have to make the decision that sleep is your priority and it conquers everything else. Often you have to make sacrifices socially (like leaving parties or social gatherings early) and you have to watch your baby like a hawk in order to spot the sleep signals.

However, by keeping on red alert you will notice any sleep signals, as mentioned in the previous chapter, and be able to take your baby upstairs for a nap in perfect timing.

Warning: When you notice the sleep signals late, it can be more challenging to put your baby to sleep. They'll be overtired, which means cortisol (the stress hormone) is coursing through their bodies.

It's good to persevere in these moments as your baby still needs to sleep - no matter how much they're protesting! By finally getting them off to sleep it will be easier to get back on schedule and you'll see a much happier baby at the next nap.

11

Five Month Old Schedule

Example of a five month old sleep schedule:

7 a.m. - Wake up

7.45 a.m. - First nap (45 minutes)

9.40 a.m. - Second nap (2 hours)

12.50 p.m. - Third nap (1 hr 40 minutes)

3.50 p.m. - Fourth nap (45 minutes)

6.05 p.m. - Bedtime

While it is SO helpful to have example sleep schedules, remember that every baby is different and every day is different. You will find a natural rhythm with your baby and learn to change their routine slightly as they grow and develop.

For example, at five months my second daughter often showed sleep signals just thirty minutes after waking up in the morning.

At first, I thought this was way too soon but I took her up for a nap anyway. She was in her cot after just thirty five minutes of being awake.

But it worked. She was happily asleep by forty five minutes with no crying whatsoever. I had found her sleep window!

In order to achieve perfect timing too, all you need to do is keep looking for your baby's sleep signals and when you see a couple of them, don't delay, take your baby up to their cot and begin the shortened wind down routine immediately.

RECAP: Wind down routine

The wind down routine takes place in a dark, cool, silent and safe room (read chapter six for full details or get a free taster of the Abundant Baby sleep video course at pages.abundantbaby.com).

You put your baby in their sleeping bag and offer them milk (if you're bottle feeding only do this if it meets your schedule of feeding), cuddle and then pop them down in their cot.

Say the same words you always say. For example, 'it's nap time now. Time to sleep.' Finally, leave the bedroom and put the music on.

At this stage a lot of babies sleep a shorter amount of time for their first nap and much longer stretches of time for the second and third nap.

The only rule in terms of nap length at five months is, the last nap of the day can only be forty five minutes at the very longest.

You are building up sleep pressure throughout the day

A shorter final nap will enable your baby to sleep deeper and longer at night. When the last nap of the day is the shortest, it helps to build sleep pressure. Your baby will be a little bit more tired without pushing it too far.

You will create a fine balance between being tired but not overtired. This sleep pressure will enable them to sleep for much longer periods of time at night.

The awake time (the time your baby is awake between sleeps) should be the longest between the final nap of the day and bedtime.

Your baby should be awake for a shorter amount of time at the start of the day and this will be lengthened throughout the day.

For example, if your baby begins by only being awake for forty five minutes between getting up in the morning and their first nap of the day then they could end the day by being awake for an hour and a half between their final nap and bedtime.

For simple explanations and worksheets get a free taster of the full extended video course at pages.abundantbaby.com. This includes a sleep table to show exactly how the awake times work throughout the day.

At this age, your baby should not be awake for longer than an hour and a half at any point during the day. Any longer and they will become overtired for sure!

Some babies will only be able to be awake for half an hour, like my daughter, at the start of the day, pushing to over an hour before bedtime.

And some babies will be able to stay awake for longer. You

will learn what is right for your baby with the help of this book and your own experience as a parent.

And remember, sleep promotes sleep

Don't feel silly if you're constantly putting your baby down for a nap. As long as they're getting up and having an awake window where they feed and interact with you, it doesn't matter how short the awake window is.

Just make sure you increase it slightly throughout the day relative to how much your baby can cope with, to ensure their sleep pressure is built. So increase by ten or fifteen minutes each time between naps but no more.

RECAP

Three to four months: Let your baby guide you. Watch out for sleep signals and put them into their cot straight away as soon as they show two or more sleep signs.

Four to six months: At five months, a routine will naturally become established and you'll start to see that each day does begin to follow the routine you have created.

Even as you let sleep signs rule and put your baby to sleep whenever they show signs of tiredness, a loose schedule will materialise. A more set routine of three -four naps will begin to emerge.

The awake time should be set in stone

The only thing that should be set in stone at this age is the awake time of your baby at the start of the day because even at three months you can begin to gently introduce the fact that your baby will always get up at the same time.

A consistent wake time is important for the circadian rhythm and will help your baby sleep peacefully at bedtime. Choose a wake up time for the day which suits you and your baby. For example, if you have chosen seven a.m. then stick to it. ALWAYS.

If your baby has a lie in, you should wake them gently to ensure they're still waking up for the day at the same time.

They may be tired and go back to sleep after half an hour but that's fine because you have started the day already.

By sticking to your wake up time, you will ensure your baby's circadian rhythm works beautifully, which will make bedtime easier for everyone.

12

How Breastfeeding Works With Sleep

Breastfeeding helps your baby to relax and feel drowsy. It puts you in control of your feeding.

You can use intuitive feeding, which means whenever your baby shows signs of being hungry during the day, you feed them.

Trust your baby. They know when they're hungry and they know when they're full.

There's nothing you need to monitor or think about when breastfeeding. In fact, the less you think about it, the better because you'll be more relaxed.

Worrying about how much milk you have or how much your baby is getting (is natural!) but it will make you feel stressed.

When you feel stressed your body inhibits the release of oxytocin which is needed to widen your milk ducts and allow milk to flow freely during breastfeeding. This is what affects the quality and quantity of your milk.

So, trust that your body is wonderful and it knows exactly what to do. Don't doubt yourself.

All you have to do is focus on getting plenty of rest, drinking lots of water and eating yummy nutritious food.

Foods which could increase breast milk quality and quantity

- Oats
- Wholegrain/wholemeal pasta
- Brown basmati rice
- Wholemeal homemade bread
- Fresh fruit and vegetables
- No alcohol

How to relax when breastfeeding

- Don't compare yourself to anyone else. Celebrate what *you* are doing and take time for yourself everyday (I know this is challenging with a baby but grab a moment when they're asleep to do something for yourself like having a nap, watching your favourite tv programme or painting your nails. Anything that makes you feel good and is something personal for you)
- Use coconut oil or natural nipple cream to avoid pain from dry nipples
- Have as much skin on skin time as possible with your baby. This stimulates breast milk flow and is a wonderful time to bond
- Don't worry about measuring milk or anything like that just offer your baby milk as much as you can and get as many cuddles as possible together

At the three month stage you can continue to be the umbilical cord for your baby as you have done for the first three months of their lives.

This is when you feed your baby on demand throughout the day whenever they show signs of being hungry. If in doubt, feed them. They will push away if they're not hungry.

Cluster feeding

Cluster feeding or bunch feeding is when your baby wants to eat frequently in short bursts at a time. This can happen during growth spurts or in the evening or simply when they need more reassurance.

Often in the evening, your baby may want to feed loads. Both my daughters would want to feed multiple times with only thirty or so minutes in-between feeding. This is natural and totally fine. I like to see it as your baby getting all their calories in before they go to sleep.

At three months, they will still wake up a lot at night. However, at four or five months you may find that your baby can go to sleep at six in the evening, wake up a few hours later for a feed and then sleep for a few more hours and have a final feed before sleeping a longer stretch of time of six or more hours (hopefully this is when you're asleep too and you can get what feels like a short but good night's sleep!)

If you've sorted out your baby's sleep crutches this is more likely. They'll be full and so when they wake up briefly in the same environment they fell asleep in, they'll be more likely to go back to sleep.

Hopefully you can both enjoy what feels like a full night's sleep of six or more hours.

If you do want to feed less at night, you can have a cut off time

When your baby is older and getting closer to the six month mark, clear feeding times will have materialised. This means you can forget about the Stop, Look and Listen night time technique and create a cut off time instead.

For example, anytime before midnight try feeding your baby immediately as soon as they wake up. By responding super quickly there is no time for your baby to cry, which means they don't release the stress hormone, cortisol (which acts as coffee to their brain and wakes them up).

This way they will stay relaxed and happy. They know their milk is nearby and they know all is good. They can then sleep for a longer stretch of time of six hours or more feeling full and happy.

Hopefully you will be able to sleep at eleven or twelve and get a full, if short, night's sleep. Your baby is now at the right age to do this so you are not taking a risk at all by letting them sleep for six hours.

Keep focused on feeding your baby throughout the day and less at night

Aim for your baby to receive seventy percent of their milk throughout the day and thirty percent at night so they can continue to learn that food is for the day and not at night.

If your baby is used to the opposite and eats less during the day and more at night, don't worry. This is common for a lot of parents.

You can adjust your baby's feeding habits by making sure you are readily available during the day. Whenever your baby shows signs of hunger, feed them.

At night, be much slower to act. Prioritise cuddling your baby over feeding them. As you gradually increase their feeds during the day, their night time feeds will reduce to a more manageable and healthy amount.

V

6 - 9 Months

Your baby is getting older and reaching major milestones! It's an exciting time but it can be disruptive to sleep. Read on to find out how to ensure you both get the sleep you need.

13

Six Month Sleep Regression

Your baby can now sleep for longer stretches of time and will only wake up once or twice at night. Things should be getting easier and hopefully it will feel like there is light at the end of the sleep deprived tunnel!

However, if you're wondering what I'm talking about and sleep has actually got worse for you at this stage, then you have joined me at the right time.

There is help available. This chapter will help you to remove unknowingly created sleep crutches.

Here's what happened with me

The four month sleep regression with my first daughter was the toughest because I didn't even know what regressions were at that point. It made things worse and so confusing because I had no idea what was going on. It was the most challenging time of my motherhood journey so far.

But in the end, it was this struggle that gave me the most hope because by six months I ended up learning loads about sleep and from that I created a sleep routine which delivered twelve hours of sleep for both my first daughter and my second daughter every single time.

Basically, this intense struggle brought a lifetime of ease.

And the same can be for you. If you're going through the same thing, know that everything will be sorted soon. Things are about to get easier. You can learn how to create a foundation for excellent sleep and you can start today.

There is one issue and one issue only

Sure, you'll face lots of different issues on the road to twelve hours of sleep for you and your baby and while teething, separation anxiety and common colds can disrupt sleep, they are (thank goodness!) temporary.

If you have created the right foundation and have eliminated the only permanent obstacle to sleep, you will get through all of these setbacks with only minor disturbances to your sleep.

What is the only permanent obstacle to sleep?

The only permanent obstacle begins at four months but is often not noticed until six months of age. This obstacle is called object permanence. Object permanence is the only thing we have to sort out in order to get perfect sleep!

If your baby is waking up every forty five minutes

If your baby won't go to sleep when you leave the room, or if you put your baby down and they instantly wake up and want you, object permanence is the reason.

Starting from as early as four months and as late as seven months, your baby acquires the skill of object permanence.

This means they are now able to remember objects when they're not there. For example, if they don't have their favourite soft toy with them they now know that this soft toy exists and so they will miss it and cry for it.

Up until this moment, your baby thought that if something wasn't with them it did not exist. Their brains were not able to recognise that something still existed even when it was out of sight.

That's why separation anxiety comes in at this age

Your baby can wake up, know that what they had before is gone but more importantly, *know* they can get it back so they will cry to get it back. This is called object permanence.

Object permanence can affect your baby's sleep because they will miss the situation they fell asleep in and want it back.

SO, let's talk about how to address this and how easy it can be to solve this issue.

Your baby will wake up many times throughout the night. This is natural. This is what adults do. We wake up, turn over and go back to sleep. Sometimes we're not even aware we've woken up.

This is the exact reason why some babies wake up every forty five minutes. Your baby is unhappy with the situation they briefly woke up in which makes them unable to fall back to sleep.

They want to recreate the exact way they initially fell asleep. For example, if you cuddled your baby to sleep and you're not there when they wake up, they'll search for you.

How do you put your baby to sleep at nap times?

Take a moment now to go over exactly what you do. Write it down. Include everything. It's important to know exactly what happens at nap time so you can find out specifically what your baby is trying to recreate when they wake up crying.

Be honest. No one will see your notes but you, so include everything that happens. Take your time to remember every last detail.

For example, your nap time routine might be far from relaxing. Like most of us, nap time can end in chaos. You may find you're patting or rocking your baby to sleep while they cry and fight sleep. You might even be crying too (I know I always was)!

Perhaps it's more peaceful than this and you're feeding your baby to sleep. They don't cry but when you put them down in the cot they'll wake up after what feels like a few seconds and immediately cry for you.

Any situation is fine - just write it down. All you have to do in this moment is know exactly what happens so you can take control and change it into a situation which will help you and your baby.

What do you do at bedtime?

Next, analyse bedtime. Is it similar to nap time? What do you do in the lead up before bedtime? Do you play with your baby? Go for a walk? Perhaps friends and family are over or the TV is on. Write down exactly what happens thirty minutes before bed.

Next, detail your wind down routine. You might not have one. Or you might have a long one which involves a bath, even a baby massage and a book.

Write everything down and then go to chapter six to create the ideal sleep routine or download a free taster of the Abundant Baby sleep course at pages.abundantbaby.com

This sleep routine should replace all nap and bedtime routines, should always happen and should never be changed.

Let's talk about how you will introduce your new routine to your baby

As your baby gets older, introducing new routines will be more challenging because, like everyone, your baby becomes used to their habits and doesn't want them to change.

Even if you're not aware you have a routine, you probably do!

This is because you will have ended up doing a similar thing every day before sleep, which means an accidental routine has taken shape.

For example, rocking your baby to sleep while they fight sleep is actually a routine because it happens everyday and your baby has become used to it.

Stick to it

The second thing to do after recording everything that happens at nap and bedtimes, is to make a decision.

Commit to the process that you are about to begin and know there is no going back.

You cannot start a new sleep programme and after a few days, try something else or give up. This will confuse your baby and massively impair sleep progress.

Before you begin implementing any changes:

- Discuss with your partner or a friend
- Make sure it is a good time to start a new routine (it is easier to do this when there are no upcoming holidays or big events)
- Take your time to read this book thoroughly
- Do your own research
- Watch my video course carefully if you prefer video content

You can get the full extended Abundant Baby Sleep course at pages.abundantbaby.com

Each module provides in-depth tutorials on introducing a new sleep routine, what to expect, how to overcome sleep barriers like separation anxiety, introducing solids and major milestones and how to do this successfully to ensure twelve hours of sleep for both you and your baby. Because ultimately that is the goal!

14

Six Month Schedule

Example of a six month nap schedule:

6.15 a.m. - Wake

8 a.m. - First Nap (1 hour)

11 a.m. - Second Nap (2 Hours)

3.15 p.m. - Third Nap (45 minutes)

6.45 p.m. - Bedtime

At six months a baby should get a total of 12 - 15 hours of sleep a day/night

This is my second daughter's exact sleep schedule at the beginning of six months when she was still breastfeeding exclusively.

She had three naps a day and could only stay awake for one hour and forty five minutes at the start of the day. She would then have a first nap which would last one hour. She would then be awake for two hours (fifteen minutes longer than her last awake time).

After that, she would have a long nap of two hours and be able to stay awake for two hours and fifteen minutes before her final and shortest nap of the day.

Her final awake time between the final nap and bed time was her longest at two hours and forty five minutes which built up sleep pressure and gave her a higher chance of sleeping through the night or only waking up once and sleeping for at least six or seven hours at a stretch.

As your baby gets older they will be able to stay awake for longer between naps

At this age you can expect your baby to be happily awake during the day for anything from an hour and half to two hours. They may be able to stay awake for one hour at the start of the day and for as long as three hours at the end of the day.

Awake times

- **First awake time** (between waking up and first nap) – 1 hr and 45 minutes
- **Second awake time** (between first and second nap) – 2 hours
- **Third awake time** – 2 hours and 15 minutes
- **Final awake time** (before bedtime) – 2 hours and 45 minutes

All babies are different. Some will get tired after an hour and a half. And some will be able to stay up for two hours even at their first wake window. Keep your eye on the sleep signals and when you see the slightest sign of your baby being tired, take them up to bed.

Sleep signals reminder

- Fussy
- Crying
- Restless
- Staring into space
- Clingy
- Slowing down

When you nail the awake windows it's pure gold! You'll experience a peaceful nap time routine every time and it will be truly brilliant.

As you practice you'll find it easier. Wake windows can be fragile. If you get it wrong even by fifteen minutes your baby could get overtired, cry and refuse to sleep.

Please don't be harsh on yourself if this happens. It's so easy to miss the perfect sleep window. A change in your baby's schedule or a change in their normal day means they can easily get overstimulated.

So, if you know your baby's day will be different to normal (perhaps you're going to a new baby group or seeing family) it's a good idea to take your baby up to nap fifteen or twenty minutes earlier than you normally would.

This means you'll avoid overstimulation and catch their sleep window perfectly.

NOTE: The very beginning of six months will be similar to the sleep schedule at the start of this chapter. However, things will change quickly as your baby grows and develops.

The six - nine month age bracket comes with big changes as this is when your baby will drop their third nap.

Some babies will be ready to do this at six or seven months while other babies may not be ready until eight or nine months.

How do you know when to drop the third nap?

This is all depends on your baby's wake times. If you see your baby is able to stay awake longer and longer and this is a natural progression, not something that was prompted by you, it may be time to drop the third nap.

Signs to watch out for when dropping the third nap

- Your baby is between six and nine months of age
- You have been observing your baby for seven days or more
- You have been watching out for sleep signals and realise your baby is simply not tired or ready for their third nap

- They consistently fight the third nap
- They stay awake happily showing no signs of distress

If your baby has started to fight the third nap consistently (everyday for seven days or more) and they seem genuinely happy to stay awake with no need to sleep, it is safe for you to drop the third nap.

15

Rapid Changes at Eight Months Old

Example of a eight month nap schedule (with two naps)

6 a.m. - Wake

8.30 a.m. - First Nap (1 hour and 30)

12.30 p.m. - Second Nap (2 hours)

6 p.m. - Bedtime

At 7 – 8 months a baby should get a total of 12 – 15 hours of sleep a day/night

The wake times are much longer now, starting with a two and a half hour awake time in the morning and stretching to as long as three and a half hours before bedtime.

If three and a half hours of awake time feels like too much to you at this early stage in your baby's life be aware that I worked with two and half hours because my baby was much more comfortable with this and then spent the rest of the time winding her down.

Example of making 3.5 hours of awake time work

2.30 p.m.- Wake from the final nap of the day

5 p.m. - Reach 2.5 hours of being awake. If your baby is happy you can now stretch to another 15 minutes

5.15 p.m.- Take your baby up to bed to wind down. Do the bedtime routine as slowly as possibly.

5.45 p.m.- Put your baby down in their cot to process their day and fall asleep

6 p.m - Your baby will now be completely asleep

So, half an hour is spent doing the bedtime wind down, then you place your baby in their cot and give them a final fifteen minutes to be in the dark happily processing their day and independently falling asleep.

Using the sleep schedule above to work from, you will now, over the next few weeks, naturally create a sleep schedule of your own that works specifically for you and your baby. You will probably make small tweaks here and there. For example, if your baby can be awake for longer this will reflect in your schedule.

When this personal sleep schedule is established, you'll find that your baby won't like to deviate!

If a sudden change happens or their wake window is too long for a reason out of your control, you'll know about it. And that's when you won't get such a peaceful nap or bedtime sleep.

NOTE: At this age you'll get a better quality of sleep if you resign yourself to the fact that an early wake time to start the day of six a.m is natural.

As long as it's not before this point, you should be fine. It's a short period of time and soon in the next few months you can work on gradually making this waking up time later and later, until seven a.m becomes the norm.

I fought this so much with my first born but relaxed the second time, knowing the six a.m. wake up time doesn't last for long.

At this age your baby is rapidly developing

Keep your eye on them and don't take wake windows for granted. The amount of time your baby can stay awake for will constantly be changing at this age.

Below is an example of how your schedule can change even in a matter of a few weeks.

As you can see, both naps are fifteen minutes later so I'm purposefully stretching the awake times because I know my baby is able to do this and it will get me closer to my preferred wake up time of seven a.m.

Example of a 8.5 month old sleep schedule

6.15 a.m. - Wake

8.45 a.m. - First Nap (1 hr and 30)

12.45 p.m. - Second Nap (2 hours)

6 p.m - Bedtime

Keep working on this by adjusting awake times and constantly adapting to your baby's rapid growth and development at this age.

16

How Do Solids Affect Sleep?

Mothers are often encouraged to put their babies on solids at three or four months old. At this stage it can feel like your baby is getting super hungry and milk is simply not enough for them but there's a lot of research which shows babies don't get their nutrients from solids at the very start. It's all about the milk.

So, by moving onto solids too quickly you aren't satisfying your baby's hunger because they're still getting most of their nutrients from milk.

In the first two months of weaning all you're doing is giving your baby a taste - a taste of lots of amazing food so they form this wonderful connection with food at an early age.

There really is no point starting a baby on solid food at three months because it will affect their sleep negatively and won't fill them up. All it will do is put more pressure on the digestive system and disturb sleep.

Wait until six months of age

Both my daughters had a massive appetite and would even lunge for food. They were displaying all the signs of being ready for solids at five months but I still preferred to wait until six months.

It meant they were totally ready and it was an easy process. It also meant their sleep was minimally affected.

At five or six months, your baby will be able to deal with the introduction of solids more easily. However, it can often still cause sleep disturbances.

So, here are three rules which should help your baby to adapt to this new addition to their life.

How do you introduce solid food without disturbing sleep?

Here are three rules you can follow for great sleep and happy weaning:

1. Let your baby try new foods for the first time at lunchtime (not dinnertime - the final meal of the day). A cut off of 1 p.m. works. It takes a long time for your baby to digest food, especially if you're introducing meat at this stage. Do it at lunchtime don't do it in the evening.
2. Your baby's food should work around their naps. At six months, babies should be given food 40 – 60 minutes before a nap to allow time to digest. As they get older this time can be reduced because their digestive system will mature and it will take a shorter amount of time to digest food. They will also be used to solid foods.

3. The last meal of the day should be at least one hour before bedtime. Even if the last meal consists of food which your baby is used to, there needs to be a cut off of at least an hour, ideally an hour and a half, before bedtime where there is no food. This is because your baby is going to have milk anyway at this stage so you don't want them going to bed with an overly full stomach because they could feel uncomfortable and overly stimulated as they try to digest their food.

Example of a six - eight month sleep and solid food schedule

6 a.m. - Wake and milk

7 a.m. - Breakfast (solids)

8.30 a.m. - First nap and milk (1 hour and 30)

11.30 a.m. - Lunch (solids)

12.30 p.m. - Second nap and milk (2 hours)

4 p.m. - Dinner (solids)

5.15 p.m. - Wind down (begin with milk)

6 p.m. - Bedtime (asleep)

NOTE: Milk may differ if you're bottle feeding so follow your normal times of feeding.

17

How to Preserve Your Sleep Routine On Holiday

The truth is, travelling will come with compromises. However, as you're completely in control of your baby's sleep programme now, you can choose what compromises to take.

The best place for your baby to sleep is their cot

Having a travel sleep plan before a holiday can be really useful. While there will be compromises, which could mean your baby's sleep will temporarily be affected, knowing this beforehand will help you to know what to do and help to minimise disruptions as much as possible.

For example, if you're about to embark on a car journey, your baby may need extra sleep when they arrive at their destination.

A lot of babies sleep well in cars (my first didn't but that's a story for another day!) but while the constant movement can lull your baby to sleep, it also stops them from entering the deep and restorative phase, which is crucial for development.

Your baby will be more tired after a car nap compared to a cot nap so, if possible, make sure your baby has had their first nap of the day at home before setting off on holiday.

This way you'll know they've had at least one deep sleep for the day.

I like to get ready and pack while they're sleeping as it's always easier doing it alone. You're probably much more organised than me, though and have already packed a week before!

Aim to be completely ready to go by the time your baby wakes up from their nap. This will give you the longest time possible in the car with a happy baby.

If the car journey is long, enjoy the time when your baby is happily awake

As their nap time approaches, stretch your baby's wake window by an extra twenty minutes because they will find it challenging to sleep in this new environment. If they're extra tired they're less likely to fight.

I know this goes against the normal rule of avoiding over-tiredness but traveling brings a lot of changes. I have witnessed my babies going to sleep a full hour after they normally would in a car.

If your baby is still breastfeeding or bottle feeding it makes sense to feed them before you attempt a nap and of course, change their nappy.

So, park up, get everything done and then get back on the road, knowing your baby is happy and ready to sleep.

Next, pop the wind down music on. This is perfect because it's the music your baby always has and so they'll feel instantly comforted and alerted to the fact that it is sleep time.

You are attempting to replicate your baby's sleep environment so make the car as dark as possible, play the lullaby music and don't interact with them.

Be flexible

You may have to have a nap on the go or drop the nap completely. You'll never normally hear me say this! But whilst travelling you can relax your sleep routines.

Attempt to replicate and give your baby the opportunity to sleep but if after thirty minutes it is simply not happening, don't worry, turn the music off if you like and continue the normal atmosphere in the car.

Often, your baby will end up falling asleep anyway. And the truth is, while I'm normally strict with sleep, you have made the choice to travel with your baby so there *are* going to be compromises.

If you managed to do the first nap of the day at home, at least you can relax knowing they have slept already. So, don't push it or stress about this second nap.

The funny thing is, sometimes when I gave up on naps in the car and stopped worrying, my baby would finally fall asleep.

Perhaps it's because I'd let go of the idea and relaxed about it. My baby could sense the decreased worry in the car and was able to fall asleep at her own pace.

NOTE: Really, the most important thing to do while travelling is to relax and know that things will be different and that that's OK. It's only temporary.

Put your baby to bed early or give them an extra nap when they arrive

When you arrive at your destination, give your baby ten minutes to see their new location, explore a little and start to get used to it and then if they haven't slept in the car, put them to sleep straight away. They'll be relieved to get in their travel cot.

Follow your sleep routine exactly as you normally would. Go to abundantbaby.com/sleep to get the full extended sleep course if you would rather see a detailed version of this module in video format.

Timings

- **If you arrive at your destination at 3 p.m. or earlier:** Put your baby to sleep for 45 minutes and then put them to sleep at their normal bedtime.
- **If you arrive at 4pm or later:** Skip the nap but begin the wind down routine for bed time 45 minutes earlier than you normally would so your baby ends up going to sleep for the night 45 minutes earlier then their regular bedtime.

I know putting your baby to bed for the night forty five minutes earlier than normal sounds insane and makes you think you'll be getting up terribly early the next morning but it works!

If your baby has missed out on a nap and they're in a new environment it stands to reason they'll be way more tired and overstimulated than normal.

And the truth is, they won't wake up earlier the next morning. They'll have an amazing night sleep and feel refreshed in the morning.

It's important to catch their tiredness and get them to sleep. You don't want your baby to get to a point where they cannot sleep because they're massively overtired.

The beauty of your sleep routine is while you may have to make a compromise when you're physically travelling (in a car, etc) when you get to your location even if it's a new place and a new sleeping environment, you will have brought along everything that is familiar for your baby.

You will have the sleeping bag, the music and the black out blind and this will create great comfort.

Keep as much as you can the same

You can proceed with your wind down routine and schedules as if you were at home.

This will work wonderfully because your baby will, as if by clockwork, follow everything you have set up. They'll be comforted by the familiarity and naturally keep to their sleep routine as they always do.

They'll be grateful of this routine. It will ground them and help them to get the best out of their holiday.

VI

9 - 12 Months

Your first wonderful year together is nearly over! It's been a blur but hopefully you are on your way to twelve hours of sleep every night.

18

Example Sleep Schedules for 9 - 10 Months Old

Your baby is now physically able to sleep through the night. Yay! Let's begin by looking at nap schedules to give a general idea of how much your baby should be sleeping at this age.

So, at eight months old a baby should have a total of twelve - fifteen hours of sleep a day (around two -three during the day and the rest at night). This is the same for a nine month baby.

However, at ten months old, while the structure is similar, your baby's wake times will increase and they will gradually start to wake up later at the start of the day, moving closer to the coveted seven a.m. wake up.

Nine Month Sleep Schedule

6.15 a.m. - Wake

9 a.m. - First Nap (1 hour and 15 mins)

1.15 p.m. - Second Nap (1 hour and 15 mins)

6.15 p.m. - Bedtime

Ten Month Sleep Schedule

6.30 a.m. - Wake

9.30 a.m. - First Nap (1 hour and 15 mins)

1.45 p.m. - Second Nap (1 hour and 15 mins)

6.30 p.m. - Bedtime

As your baby gets older you should start to see awake times of as long as three hours, sometimes three and a half. All babies are different. Some may be able to stay awake for longer while others not, however what is for sure is that these awake times are increasing.

So, even if your baby started off at three months with forty five minutes of awake time they will now have reached three hours in the morning and will still increase by fifteen minute increments throughout the day, building the sleep pressure for the night with the longest wake time at the end of the day.

Don't drop the second nap too soon

When your baby comes into the eleven month age bracket, you may think it's time to drop the second nap. This is because your baby starts resisting it.

However, beware! This is often not a sign to drop the second nap at all. It's usually just an indication that your baby can now stay awake for longer in-between naps.

So, if your baby is fighting naps and you're giving them a three hour window, increase this to three hours and fifteen minutes and then to three hours and thirty minutes over the space of a week.

If you're already at three and half hours, don't worry you can still increase by fifteen minutes to three hours and forty five minutes.

Some babies prefer a shorter awake time of three hours and fifteen minutes and some can be awake for longer.

If the timings are confusing check out the full extended sleep video course at abundantbaby.com/sleep for clear video tutorials, specific timings and charts.

Often everything feels slower and clearer on a video. Plus, worksheets are available as part of the course which you can keep and check at any point.

Keep observing the sleep signs

The only way you'll know what suits your baby is by observing their sleep signs.

If when you take them to bed, they're crying and protesting and seeming stressed then they're overtired and need a shorter awake time.

On the other hand, if your baby is relatively happy but simply not sleeping then they're undertired and can stay awake for longer.

REMINDER: If your baby starts resisting the second nap, don't drop it. They're not ready yet.

Dropping the second nap doesn't happen until fourteen – eighteen months. This is not a sign to drop the second nap. It is a sign to stretch the time your baby is awake between naps by fifteen minutes a day.

11 – 12 Month Sleep Schedule

6.45 a.m. - Wake

10 a.m. - First Nap (1 hour and 15 mins)

2.30 p.m. - Second Nap (1 hour and 15 mins)

7.15 p.m. - Bedtime

19

What to Do if Your Baby Starts Standing Up or Crawling in Their Cot

Milestones are an exciting and amazing time in your baby's life. They have a newfound freedom and strength.

While this is truly wonderful to observe and the funnest time (my first born used to run instead of walking with her hands in the air and my second crawled at such a speed it was impressive!)

While it's an exciting time, new skills can cause disruptions to sleep. So, let's talk about when these milestones happen and how to cope with them.

Major Milestones

6 months – A baby will be able to roll over both ways

9 months - Most babies can crawl, some will be pulling themselves up to stand and a few may even be cruising at this stage (walking while holding onto furniture, etc)

12 months - Some babies can walk at this stage, others are still practising and crawling confidently

15 months - Most babies can walk at this point

These are general indications. Some babies are earlier with their milestones and other babies are later.

It can feel stressful, especially with your first born and especially if you have parents around you with babies who are rolling before yours or crawling happily when your baby is content to not even try, but the truth is, they'll get there in the end. All babies do.

It isn't a competition (even though it can feel like it sometimes!) your baby may simply prefer to observe everyone else first and then crawl or walk confidently when their time is right.

I couldn't wait for each milestone. I was so excited to see my baby crawl. But the truth is, I quickly realised that reaching milestones early is the end of your peace. No longer will your baby relax on their baby mat looking at their sheep mobile or cuddle in your arms without wanting to jump up and get going.

You'll have to childproof your house and run around in a frenzy keeping your precious new toddler safe. It's a great time but a busy time!

So, don't worry if your baby is slower to reach these milestones. It could be better for your sleep and peace overall!

NOTE: However, if you are at all concerned about reaching milestones, consult your doctor to put your mind at ease.

New skills can temporarily disturb sleep

As you would expect, your baby will want to practice their newfound skill. Anywhere and everywhere! They'll take longer to fall asleep or even wake up in the middle of the night to practice.

This is common near the end of the nine month age bracket when some babies start trying to stand up in their cots.

While this is fun for your baby, it can be scary for you because it increases the chance of accidents happening.

They could fall in their cots while attempting to stand or bang into the sides while crawling. Both my children constantly barreled into the sides of their cots, which was horrifying to witness!

Newfound skills pose a big challenge. If your baby is constantly pulling themselves up to stand or crawling about in their cot, you'll naturally want to go in to their bedroom to check they're OK.

Suddenly, your watertight sleep routine is disrupted. It's impossible to leave your baby to process their day alone in their cot if you cannot guarantee their safety.

So, how do we solve this?

Babies are incredible. They're always looking to see how they can get stronger in order to survive. When they're a newborn they feed and sleep all the time in order to grow bigger.

When they reach six - twelve months of age, things change. Now, their best chance for strength and development is to get mobile.

The quicker they're independent with their mobility, the better it is for them. Hence, why they constantly practice crawling, standing and walking.

Four things to do to help your baby sleep during each milestone

- **Give your baby lots of time to practice during the day** - this mean they won't feel tempted to practice at night. Include lots of time on the floor, making sure you have cleared the space so there's nothing your baby can reach for or pull down on themselves. A play pen does work but an open space of floor is freer and provides more room to move and explore in
- **Baby proof your house** - in order for your baby to have true freedom of movement and feel like the space is their own, baby proof your whole house and watch your baby closely as they roll and crawl. This independence will increase their confidence. I prefer to use one room at a time as it feels safer and easier
- **When your baby attempts to practice skills at sleep time be gentle, firm and consistent** - if you're putting your baby down to sleep and they instantly stand up or start rolling about inside their cot, pat them and say, 'lie down it's sleep time now'.
- **Stick to your original sleep programme** - even though it can seem impossible when your baby keeps pulling themselves up on their cot, sticking to your original plan and not deviating will keep sleep disturbance to a minimum (go to pages.abundantbaby.com to get a free taster of the

full extended baby sleep video course to find out exactly how to do this).

Keep your tone gentle but firm

Do not interact more than you need to. By sticking to your original sleep plan, you tell your baby that it is sleep time and not play time. Keep putting your baby back down gently in their cot with the same soothing sleep time words.

You can, of course, be flexible with milestones. So, while at sleep time you're aiming to leave the room and stay outside, at first you may want to be in the room more because understandably you could be concerned about your baby's safety as they practice their new skills.

That's totally natural and absolutely fine. Don't rush or try to leave the room before you feel at peace with your baby's environment.

Allow yourself extra time in the room to ensure you're happy

Every time your baby attempts to practice their new skills, put them gently back down, using the same sleep words.

Keep the room dark and everything the same as the routine always is. Then when you are finally happy, leave the room.

When you're outside you may feel the need to listen more closely and if you hear your baby bang into the sides of the cot or hurt themselves, obviously go straight back in to check they're OK.

However, if you can hear that your baby is crawling or rolling about and they're happy, leave them in peace to process their day.

Some babies are so eager to practice that no matter how much time you give them during the day they'll still do more at sleep time.

Practising skills can be a way of processing the day

Practising can also be a way of processing so, as long as your baby is happy and safe, it's fine. You could temporarily wait outside for longer to ensure they don't hurt themselves.

And remember this phase doesn't last long. It's such a small and brief moment in your baby's life. Before you know it, these new skills will become old ones and your baby will be happy to go straight to sleep. The novelty factor will have worn off.

Stick to your sleep programme no matter what

Give your baby plenty of time to practice during the day and keep consistent at sleep time with the same environment, same sleep time words and same soothing, gentle tone. Keep that consistency and your baby will learn from you.

A lot is changing. They're seeing for the first time how much the world can give them. With all these big changes in their life, keeping your baby's sleep routine exactly the same will give them a great source of security and confidence.

20

Lengthening the Wake Windows Without Overstimulation

The wonderful thing about the nine – twelve month age bracket is your wake windows are getting so much longer. They could be anything from three hours to three hours and forty five minutes.

That's a lot of time.

You can go to the park and back in that time. You can go to a baby class and have a coffee after. You can finally do a lot in your day!

There's suddenly time for you to do things

When your baby was three months old it probably felt like all you were doing was putting them to sleep all day.

Now it's different. You have more time. But what comes with more time is the risk of over stimulation.

So, it's really important that if you *do* go out, you leave plenty of time for your baby to wind down when you get back home. And not just enough time for their normal wind down.

Reminder: At this age for bedtime a wind down time of thirty

-forty five minutes is perfect and for nap times five– fifteen minutes is recommended.

Be careful of new baby classes or events

If you've taken your baby to a park, class or event that you don't normally go to, double your baby's wind down time.

So, instead of five – fifteen minutes before their nap time, you should be aiming for twenty – thirty minutes.

When you arrive home - slow down

If you've been rushing to get back, now is the time to relax. Give your baby a moment to settle in the house before you take them up for their nap.

They're home now. It's probably quieter and more peaceful at home than wherever you were, so allow them ten minutes to settle.

Remember what it was like when you came back from a late night and your ears were still ringing and you needed time to relax before bed! Your baby feels the same.

Next, begin the wind down routine

The best thing to do is, to spend five minutes reading a book and cuddling as per usual, but pop your baby down to sleep ten minutes earlier than you normally would and leave the room.

Allowing ten or fifteen minutes for them to chat to themselves and wind down after a stimulating day or new activity is essential.

Aim for a thirty minute wind down after anything different

The lengthened nap wind-down will look like this:

10 minutes to settle at home

10 minutes of reading a book in your baby's darkened bedroom

10 minutes for your baby to process in their cot before they fall asleep

Overstimulation at this age is the reason why your baby can sometimes cry more than normal or take longer to nap.

So, plan your times beforehand – check when events are or how long it takes to get to the park so you can allow for a longer wind down.

Even if the idea of planning ahead does not appeal to you, it's so worth it! It means you won't have an overtired baby who refuses to sleep. It makes life easier for everyone.

If you see any signs of your baby becoming tired when you're out, don't delay

Cut the event short. It doesn't matter what anyone thinks. It's just you and your baby's sleep that's important, so get back home and begin your lengthened wind down routine.

The same applies if you have hosted a social gathering in your own home - either say goodbye or let your guests know you'll be back in twenty minutes after you have done the nap wind down and put your baby to sleep.

A reminder of sleep signals to watch out for:

- Fussy
- Clingy
- Restless
- Staring into space
- Crying
- Suddenly slowing down in their activities (or speeding up!)

Cutting short an activity or leaving a social gathering early can feel like a sacrifice but it's worth it if you value your sleep.

And remember this is only for one year of your life. Once your baby reaches twelve months old, you can go to events and it won't be such a rush to get back because your baby will have less naps during the day and be able to stay awake for longer.

Summary

It's all about giving your baby time to process so they can begin to feel sleepy without being overtired.

If you put your baby down in their cot when they're getting close to a nap but are not yet ready to sleep, it will give them time to relax and process their new experience before sleeping.

This is much better than your baby getting put in their cot late for their nap as they will often then struggle to soothe themselves and seem restless.

NOTE: When a baby is overtired they become stressed. They release cortisol and adrenaline which is like coffee for their brain! This is why an overtired baby is so challenging to soothe.

21

How to Sleep Through The Night From 7pm - 7am

It's the moment you've been waiting for. Drumroll please . . .

So, how do you actually get your baby to sleep all the way through the night from seven p.m. – seven a.m.?

At this stage your baby can sleep through the night safely.

Some people say babies can sleep through the night from as early as six months old but I prefer the age bracket of nine - twelve months as there is no doubt at this point.

By nine - twelve months, a baby can healthily and happily sleep through the night every night without the dream feed and for a full twelve hours.

Don't get annoyed with yourself if your baby is still struggling with sleep at twelve months old. This is so normal!

Most parents are still struggling with sleep too. And while it can be frustrating, the good thing is you can feel confident starting your new sleep programme now because you know your baby is old enough.

You don't have to worry about them feeding at night or physically not being ready because they totally *are* ready now.

You can commit to the sleep routine with the knowledge it will work.

Three things you need to address before your baby can sleep through the night

1. Get rid of any night feeds gradually
2. Drop the dream feed
3. Push early morning wakings later

At this age your baby can sleep through the night without feeds so any night time feeds are essentially down to habit and can be healthily removed.

However, don't do this all at once. Drop them gradually. This will take commitment as it takes time and patience for your baby to get used to not eating at night.

By transitioning slowly you give your baby the opportunity to eat more calories during the day so they are not at a deficit. It gives them time to adjust and will ensure they feel happy.

Begin by writing everything down

Record every last detail -what exactly are you doing at night? What time are you putting your baby to sleep and when do their night time feeds happen?

If there is only one or two night time feedings– perfect. Leave the feed where your baby seems the hungriest to the end. This one should be the last feed to be dropped.

You will then begin to gradually decrease night time feeds

Drop one feed at a time, while observing your baby to make sure they're happy. It can feel like an impossible feat to eliminate night time feeds. For example, if you cut down feeds to a few minutes, how on earth do you get to zero (no feeds at all?) without your baby being unhappy?

There are simple tutorials on abundantbaby.com/sleep as part of the enhanced sleep course where you will find out exactly how to shorten feeds at a rate which suits your baby with worksheets to ensure this change in your baby's life goes as smoothly and successfully as possible. Happy baby, happy mama.

NOTE: At first when you implement night time changes you may feel really tired but you're already exhausted so just know that you're getting there. You're getting closer to not having to do this at all and having the effortless twelve hours of sleep that you've been working towards.

Drop the dream feed

At first, I felt worried at the idea of dropping the dream feed because it was helping me to get a solid chunk of sleep at night. I was scared my baby would wake up hungry in the night and my sleep would get worse instead of better.

However, the truth was, my sleep improved and it was the right time to drop the dream feed. So, don't worry. This is the best decision.

In fact, if you continue to dream feed past eleven months it can even disrupt your baby because you're creating a habit of eating at a specific time every night instead of sleeping through the night with no food.

Your baby will have been eating solids for months now so they no longer even need this dream feed.

However, it can act as an extra cuddle and comfort for some babies so make sure there's plenty of time for cuddles throughout the day to ensure they don't miss out on time with you.

As long as you know you're doing this, there's nothing wrong with night time weaning. It's an important time and a positive part of your baby's development.

How to drop the dream feed

If your chosen time to dream feed is eleven p.m., for example, you should now make this time thirty minutes earlier every three or four days.

Once you get to nine p.m (if you don't want to go to bed yet) instead of rolling over to go to sleep you'll just leave the room super quietly.

Keep on going until you have reached whatever time is already the last feed for your baby. This means you will have eliminated the dream feed.

And you will have done it gently and slowly over time.

It's basically like a wake window so instead of stretching a wake window, you're stretching the milk window, which is how long your baby can go without milk.

You'll know when it is right to do this. At nine or ten months your baby may still seem hungry at the dream feed but as you get closer to eleven months they'll be less hungry and the timings will be perfect.

Push early morning wakings later

The final part of sleeping from seven p.m. to seven a.m. are the early morning wakings. No more waking up at four or five in the morning!

This can be one of the most challenging parts of getting twelve hours of sleep.

The final piece of the puzzle

Pushing the early morning wakings is a similar process to dropping a feed during the night but instead of cutting down the amount of time you're feeding your baby, you're going to stretch the time you first feed them in the morning.

The reason why babies struggle to get back to sleep after an early morning feed is because their levels of melatonin (the sleep hormone) are less in these early hours than in the middle of the night.

Plus, early morning breast milk contains adrenaline and cortisol so the first feed of the day is like a cup of coffee for your baby. The later you manage to push it, the better.

Try half an hour later every morning

For example, if your baby wakes up at three in the morning, put the music on and wait half an hour.

Keep pushing the time you feed them by half an hour every two or three days.

At first, it will seem pointless because you're awake anyway and not getting your rest and your baby will be complaining about not getting their milk.

However, you're gradually getting your baby used to eating at a later time in the morning.

Remember, at this age it's all habits – they don't *need* to eat early in the morning at all. It might seem like a mission but you will reach seven a.m.

As you get closer to a normal first feed of the day – six or seven a.m. - you may find that sometimes your baby simply won't go back to sleep at all.

In this situation, don't worry. Still stretch the time for as long as you can and don't give up.

Decide the night before what time is the earliest you will consider waking up. This is a pre-planned cut off point which you won't break no matter what. For example, if you decide six a.m. is your cut off, do not feed your baby any earlier than this.

When it's time, feed your baby and start the day. Soon six a.m. will turn to seven.

As your baby gets used to having more food during the day and gets older even by just days or weeks (it's all counts for a lot at this stage) their natural wake up time will get later until you have your seven p.m. to seven a.m. official sleeping hours.

Summary

To finally achieve twelve hours of sleep from seven p.m. all the way through to seven a.m., there are four steps.

1. Record everything that currently happens at night
2. Get rid of any night time feeds gradually
3. Drop the dream feed
4. Finally push early morning wakings later by half an hour every morning until you have reached an acceptable time

You will now have twelve hours of sleep every single night. The goal you have been working towards since the beginning has been accomplished.

Your determination and consistency has paid off. By believing in yourself and committing to the sleep programme you have created twelve hours of sleep every night for your whole family.

You have helped your baby to form amazing sleep habits for life. Well done! It's a huge achievement.

VII

12 Months and Beyond

Congratulations on your first year as a parent. There are still sleep obstacles to come but hopefully you are well on your way to excellent sleep!

22

12 Month Sleep Check To Remove Sleep Crutches

Congratulations on your first year with your baby! It's such an amazing time but also an intense, tearful, challenging and emotional year full of major highs and lows. I learnt so much in my first year.

Now, if you've managed to get sleep sorted and you've been following each chapter as your baby develops and grows then absolutely amazing!

If not and you're having some issues with sleep this is really common. I don't know why it's made out that some parents have got it sussed at say, six months, as this is absolutely not the case.

> *"Only 57% of babies stay asleep for eight hours straight at the age of one year"*
>
> *- McGill University Montreal Canada*

It is completely normal to have issues with sleep. And it's not too late to change.

Sure, at this age your baby will have developed some habits and things can feel cemented.

However, the process is the same. All you have to do is introduce the ideal sleep routine from chapter one and stick to it.

Go back and read it again now.

Here's a quick wind down summary:

1. Create the ideal sleep environment – dark, cool, silent and safe
2. Keep consistent with the routine – feed, book, cuddle and into the cot
3. Say the same words. For example – 'It's sleep time now. Night, night.'
4. Leave the room and put the music on
5. Stay outside the room only going back in if you absolutely have to
6. Make the time in the room brief and keep increasing how long you wait outside the room before going back in
7. If your baby is relatively happy, let them process their day and fall asleep independently without going back into the room

12 Month Example Schedule

6.45 a.m - Wake

10 a.m - First nap (1 hour and 15 minutes)

2.30 p.m - Second nap (45 minutes)

7.15 p.m - Bedtime

Total amount of sleep needed: 12 – 14 hours

Dropping the second nap

At twelve months it's very common for parents to want to drop the second nap but this shouldn't happen until your baby gets to at least fourteen or fifteen months of age.

Often the answer to a baby constantly fighting naps isn't that they don't want to sleep anymore, it's actually that they're not tired enough but would like to sleep at a different point.

By looking at the twelve month sleep schedule above you can see that your baby's wake windows have changed dramatically. Your baby can now be awake for as long as three hours and fifteen minutes in the morning.

This should be built throughout the day, so add on fifteen minutes for the next wake time. You are aiming for your baby to be awake for as long as four hours before bedtime. This builds sleep pressure which will help your baby to sleep all night long.

What to do if your toddler protests

If this is the first time you have introduced a wind down routine and sleep schedule, you may find that your toddler will protest more.

That's fine. The truth is, they will always protest.

At three months old a baby will cry at the change in their routine and need to be soothed.

However at this age, your toddler's protests may seem more angry than sad. They want to do what they want to do. They're learning independence and they're learning that they can influence some actions in this world, which is brilliant. This is great for their confidence.

But this secure foundation of amazing sleep which you're creating for your child is so important.

And while they may feel angry that this is something they can't change, it will also benefit them. A sleep routine will give them security in an ever-changing world.

The most important thing is that you stick to it. Know that it will take time. It could take two weeks. It could even take three weeks. Don't expect this to be sorted in a few days at this age.

A lot of toddlers will even seem do the routine easily for the first day or two and then suddenly backtrack and get extra annoyed and try to fight against it. This is when you stick to what you are doing.

Do not doubt yourself

Keep going, keep comforting your toddler, keep calm and stick to the wind down routine.

Your toddler will thank you so much for it because you are not budging. You're keeping to the same routine no matter what. And this makes them feel secure and confident.

More importantly this sleep routine is not just for now. This is for life. You are teaching your toddler amazing sleep habits forever.

We all need to wind down before sleeping. And we all need to be able to sleep when we're tired. Toddlers and babies don't know how to do this so it's your job to teach them.

> *"Research shows that children who follow bedtime routines are more likely to go to sleep earlier, take less time falling asleep, sleep longer, and wake up less during the night."*
> *– The Sleep Foundation*

What Are Sleep Crutches?

If you have unknowingly introduced sleep crutches, now is the time to teach your baby how to sleep without them.

Sleep crutches are things your baby needs to fall asleep which will disrupt your sleep.

Examples include:

- Dummies
- Breastfeeding or bottle feeding
- Cuddling or patting to sleep

Your baby can't be reliant on somebody else to sleep even if it is you because that will not work for them long-term.

So, as much as you may feel that you're not being fair on your baby by introducing this new sleep routine, remember that you are. You are doing the best thing for your baby by teaching them the skill of falling asleep independently as it ultimately leads to a higher quality of sleep.

Stick to it. You're doing amazing.

For the next three weeks work on getting the ideal sleep routine completely sorted. It could take three weeks or it could take one. Every baby is different.

So, put aside three weeks and expect it to take a long time. That way it will feel like a bonus if your baby adjusts to their new sleep routine in as little as a week.

And remember, don't ever give up. You have made the commitment now. There's no going back!

23

14 Month Sleep Regression

Unfortunately it's very common to experience another sleep regression at this point. This sleep regression could happen at any point between twelve – eighteen months of age.

Now, I know this sounds like a huge window but this is because it's a very different sleep regression.

The fourteen month sleep regression is less of a regression and more of an indication that it is time to adjust your sleep schedule.

It's not like the four or eight month sleep regression which are both the result of your baby's brain changing.

No. At this point it's all about transitioning from two naps to one and understanding your baby's wake windows.

Often, a parent may not realise that their baby can stay awake for a much longer stretch of time at this age. This can cause a baby to resist their a nap, start waking up at night when they didn't before and be generally fussier.

Three signs your baby's wake times are too short

1. They have started resisting naps when they previously went to sleep peacefully
2. They have started waking up at night when they were sleeping through before
3. They are fussier and cry more than normal

The fourteen month regression is nothing to worry about. It's simply a sign you need to jig your day time routine around a bit.

Example of a fourteen month nap schedule:

7 a.m - Wake

Awake for 3 hours and 15 minutes

10.15 a.m - First nap (1 hour)

Awake for 3 hours and 15 minutes

2.30 p.m - Second nap (1 hour)

7 p.m - Bedtime (Awake for 3 hours and 30 minutes before bed)

At 14 months your child should get a total of 12 – 14 hours of sleep a day.

NOTE: If you need more help in adjusting your baby's nap schedule and knowing exactly when to drop this second nap without disrupting sleep, go to abundantbaby.com/sleep for the full video course.

The course will guide you past twelve months even as far as five years of age, dealing with further sleep regressions, nightmares and extra sleep obstacles like how to share a bedroom with a sibling and when to drop naps altogether.

24

The Biggest Obstacle to Sleep for Toddlers

Often when babies get to one, two, three or four years of age, screens become a bigger part of their life.

Unfortunately, while screens can form a positive part of parenthood, they are stimulating and will only disrupt sleep. Sure, they can be fun and educational when used correctly but they do nothing for sleep.

With this in mind, if sleep is your priority, keep screen time to a maximum of twenty minutes a day and no screens whatsoever two hours before bedtime. This includes everything - television, tablets, games and phones.

REASON: Screens emit blue light. Blue light suppresses the body's melatonin making it more challenging to fall asleep and stay asleep throughout the night.

Children are particularly sensitive to blue light as they have larger pupils.

Screens do not help sleep at all

In fact, screens have been proven to interrupt sleep. So, no screens two hours before bedtime is a rule which will massively help.

This is definitely the best thing to do if you are experiencing interrupted sleep or a new resistance to bedtime and you have no idea why. Drop screens altogether for two weeks and see if the situation improves.

Sugar can cause your toddler to wake up during the night

Studies have found that the more sugar your child eats during the day, the more times they will wake up in the middle of the night.

Even if they don't fully wake up, the sugar in their system can pull them out of a deep sleep, making them exhausted the next day and more prone to overtiredness and tantrums.

So, if your toddler SEEMS to be sleeping all night but is super tired and you don't know why, this could be because they are missing out on a deeper and more restorative sleep.

If sugar is a big part of your family life, simply try reducing by one or two treats a day and make a rule of no sugar two hours before bedtime.

No excessive loud noises

Two hours before bed make sure all screens are off. Stop any loud music and begin a gradual slowing down of the day. This will create a feeling of calm in the house.

Encourage puzzles, read or do sticker books. You can even dim the lights and create a sleepy environment. This sets the scene for bedtime.

You don't want your toddlers running around and making loud noises because this makes them feel like it's the middle of the day and nowhere near bedtime.

Some days this will be more challenging than others. And as your toddler gets older it may become pretty much impossible to get them to quieten down before bed.

The best way to do this is to have fun!

Play quiet games like, my favourite, Sleeping Fishes. Read your toddler's favourite book or talk to them quietly about something they love.

Shouting be quiet or trying to convince them to do something they don't want to do will probably not work (even though it happens to the best of us after a long day!)

By gradually slowing the day down and getting your toddler ready for bed it will be less of a shock when you say it's bedtime.

They'll be more likely to listen to you and less likely to protest because you have prepared them for sleep and gradually made them feel sleepier.

So, give your toddler a five minute warning before bed and then a two minute one afterwards. This may seem basic but it works.

Remember, your toddler has no idea what's going on unless you tell them. It helps them to feel in control and know what's coming next.

No new food or heavy meals

The final thing to avoid at this age before bedtime is new foods. As your toddler starts to get older you may be more likely to try new foods as a family.

Exploring new foods is a wonderful thing to do and it's so important in terms of increasing confidence and happiness associated with food.

However, if your toddler does this too close to their bedtime, even at the older age of three or four years of age, it could disturb their sleep.

Trying new foods or having meals too close to bedtime can increase core body temperature and stimulate digestion, which disrupts the production of the sleep hormone, melatonin.

It's worth noting that if you want to give your toddler new food during the final meal of the day, give them a tiny bit or don't bother at all and keep new food for lunch time. You don't want their digestive system to go into overdrive too close to bedtime.

Summary:

1. Try to keep high energy games and loud noises to a minimum thirty minutes before winding down
2. Keep sugar to a minimum throughout the day for a deeper, more restorative sleep and have none at all two hours before bed
3. Reduce screen time to twenty minutes during the day and cut off all screens two hours before bed
4. Avoid heavy meals or new foods one hour before bedtime

As your toddler gets older, it's wonderful because things become less strict and you can do a lot more in a day.

They're no longer a baby and you don't have to worry about rushing them home because they've been awake for half an hour and their wake window is up!

But, it's still important to be aware that your toddler can get overstimulated and things like screens and sugar massively affect this.

So, where possible, keeping screens and sugars to a minimum, helps you hugely with sleep.

Sugar, screens, new foods and extremes like loud noises or activity before bedtime are the main reasons why a toddler is not sleeping at this age, especially if you already have a sleep routine in place.

For more guidance go to pages.abundantbaby.com for a free taster of the Abundant Baby video course.

VIII

Extras

25

The Whole Book Jammed Into Four Pages

This is for the tired parent who can't keep their eyes open long enough to read a whole book!

I know how you feel.

In the first eight months of my daughter's life I couldn't understand why people expected me to take part in normal conversations or anything that required any kind of effort at all.

If you'd asked me to read a book I would have stared at you blankly, or cried. I was exhausted.

So, with this in mind, I've crammed as much as I can into the next few pages so you don't have to read this whole book.

Twelve hours of sleep could be closer than you think. Hopefully, just around the next page . . .

0 - 3 months

Chill out. Well, as much as you can when you're recovering from the most intense experience of your life, getting used to the agony of breastfeeding or bottle feeding and adjusting to life as a new parent!

BUT you get my drift. No sleep routine is needed. Your baby needs loads of sleep. Don't wake them up. Rest instead.

If you're going to do one thing in the first three months and one thing only to encourage excellent sleep habits: Go for a walk during the day with your baby when you feel able to.

This will create a clear difference between night and day for both you and your baby. And don't tiptoe around during the day either (unless you do normally). There needs to be a difference between night and day.

3 - 6 months

It's time to create the ideal sleep environment. You're going to hear this phrase from me so much but it's vital because it's the absolute foundation of excellent sleep.

The ideal sleep environment is:

- Dark
- Cool
- Silent
- Safe

So, use a black-out blind, check the temperature of the bedroom is between sixteen – twenty degrees Celsius, read the sleep safety guidelines online and play soothing music if silence is not possible.

RANDOM TIP: Brian Eno, Apollo is the best lullaby album for your baby's sleep. I used to use white noise but there have been studies that show continuous white noise can harm the brain by overstimulating the auditory cortex.

The only sleep time routine you need:

1. Nappy and t-shirt on (or no t-shirt if you live in a hot country and not rainy UK)
2. Feed your baby in the darkened environment (this only applies if you're still bottlefeeding/breastfeeding)
3. Cuddle your baby standing up - It's important not to get too comfy as you don't want them falling asleep
4. Put your baby down in their cot. Pat them and say goodnight before leaving the room
5. The aim is NOT to go back in. Feel free to wait outside the door to check they're OK
6. Only go in after thirty seconds if your baby is seriously unhappy. A little complaining is fine. Believe it or not, you can end up disrupting your baby by constantly going back in. I know thirty seconds can feel like an eternity but it is so important to give your baby a chance to wind down by themselves. You may be surprised - they could be a lot calmer after thirty seconds or they could even stop crying altogether and go to sleep
7. If you don't feel happy and want to go back in, then make sure your time in the room is brief. Pat your baby in their cot (only bringing them out to cuddle if you have to), then

choose the same words to whisper. For example, 'It's sleep time now. Sleep well. I love you' and leave the room

8. Increase to waiting for forty five seconds before going back in
9. Increase to sixty seconds and then ninety seconds. By this point your baby should be asleep or drowsy/happy. If you have to keep going in, wait for longer each time and be brief in the room. At first your baby may not be pleased with this new routine but no one likes change and in the end they will sleep beautifully and happily every time. You are doing the right thing!
10. By listening outside the door you are constantly monitoring how happy or not your child is and by soothing them when they need it, you are able to be as gentle as possible while still teaching them the skill of falling to sleep by themselves. This will, in the long run, benefit your baby as they need restorative, deep sleep in order to be happy and not disrupted sleep which relies on you.

6 - 9 months

Your baby can now remember things. This is called object permanence and can occur as early as three months.

I know what you're thinking - Object what?! But basically all you need to know is: **Your baby should be put down to sleep in the same place they wake up.**

For example, not in your arms and then switched to a cot. This will alarm them. Imagine if you fell asleep in your bed after a night out and woke up in the bath. Disconcerting, right?!

This unexpected switch of location could be causing your baby to resist sleep which is totally understandable when you see it through their perspective.

9 - 12 months

Your baby can now stay awake for longer in-between naps (anything from three hours to three hours and forty five minutes) so make sure they are awake for longer so they can build up sleep pressure before nap time and bedtime. This will help your baby to sleep through the night.

12 months+

At fourteen months your baby will be ready to drop their second nap. Monitor them for two weeks to see if they consistently fight naps and can stay awake for longer while seeming genuinely not tired. This means they're ready.

Three years +

At this age your baby is ready to drop naps altogether. But again monitor your child for two weeks to see if they're truly ready as some children prefer to keep their nap until four years of age.

Three years is also a good time to check screens, sugar and extremes before bed (extremes are loud noises, bright lights, excessive running about).

All of these things are not good for sleep so no fun or laughing before bed! (OK so I know this is an impossible rule but sitting down to colour, read or do sticker books with your toddlers before bed will encourage a calmer and more peaceful environment).

IMPORTANT NOTE: Remember this is the whole book jammed into a few pages so if it feels overwhelming, skip this part and read the whole book chapter by chapter.

By taking your time to read the whole thing, you'll find longer explanations and be able to understand each important component of getting your baby to sleep through the night at your own pace.

If you prefer video content because you can dip in and out whenever you want, go to pages.abundantbaby.com for a free taster of the step by step video course with simple worksheets and charts to help you at each stage of your baby's life (newborn all the way through to four years and older).

26

Sleep Schedules According to Your Baby's Age

Here are all the sleep schedules mentioned in this book in one place. If you need a specific age group which you cannot find here go to abundantbaby.com to find the age appropriate sleep schedule.

Five Months Sleep Schedule

7 a.m. - Wake up

7.45 a.m. - First nap (45 minutes)

9.40 a.m. - Second nap (2 hours)

12.50 p.m. - Third nap (1 hr 40 minutes)

3.50 p.m. - Fourth nap (45 minutes)

6.05 p.m. – Bedtime

Six Months Sleep Schedule

6.15 a.m. - Wake

8 a.m. - First Nap (1 hour)

11 a.m. - Second Nap (2 Hours)

3.15 p.m. - Third Nap (45 minutes)

6.45 p.m. - Bedtime

Eight Months Sleep Schedule

6 a.m. - Wake

8.30 a.m. - First Nap (1 hour and 30)

12.30 p.m. - Second Nap (2 hours)

6 p.m. - Bedtime

Eight Months Solids and Sleep Schedule

6 a.m. - Wake and milk

7 a.m. - Breakfast (solids)

8.30 a.m. - First nap and milk (1 hour and 30)

11.30 a.m. - Lunch (solids)

12.30 p.m. - Second nap and milk (2 hours)

4 p.m. - Dinner (solids)

5.15 p.m. - Wind down (begin with milk)

6 p.m. - Bedtime (asleep)

Eight Months and Half Sleep Schedule

6.15 a.m. - Wake

8.45 a.m. - First Nap (1 hr and 30)

12.45 p.m. - Second Nap (2 hours)

6 p.m - Bedtime

Nine Months Sleep Schedule

6.15 a.m. - Wake

9 a.m. - First Nap (1 hour and 15 mins)

1.15 p.m. - Second Nap (1 hour and 15 mins)

6.15 p.m. - Bedtime

Ten Months Sleep Schedule

6.30 a.m. - Wake

9.30 a.m. - First Nap (1 hour and 15 mins)

1.45 p.m. - Second Nap (1 hour and 15 mins)

6.30 p.m. - Bedtime

Eleven - Twelve Months Sleep Schedule

6.45 a.m. - Wake

10 a.m. - First Nap (1 hour and 15 mins)

2.30 p.m. - Second Nap (1 hour and 15 mins)

7.15 p.m. - Bedtime

Fourteen Months Sleep Schedule

7 a.m - Wake

10.15 a.m - First nap (1 hour)

2.30 p.m - Second nap (1 hour)

7 p.m - Bedtime

IX

SOS for Parents

This part is dedicated to those questions which seem to have no solution at all like – 'Why is my baby waking up every 45 minutes?' and 'Will I EVER sleep again?!'

Skip to the question of your choice to find a simple solution.

27

What is the Umbilical Cord Method?

The Umbilical Cord Method is basically the idea of feeding your baby as and when they want. It's feeding on demand one level up. It's where you cuddle and be with your baby all day so milk is constantly available to them.

In the womb your baby had food and sleep whenever they wanted. Now they're out on planet Earth and in your arms and suddenly they don't have food on tap anymore.

So, why not be the umbilical cord?

Give your baby milk (throughout the day!) whenever they want. This works well for breastfeeding as your baby cannot have too much. They know when they're full. It's totally fine to offer breast milk all day long to your newborn.

While this is slightly different with bottle feeding, it can still work. You will simply need to monitor the amount of milk your baby has more closely and make sure you keep to the recommended amounts of formula.

Feeding your baby on tap throughout the day means that

when it comes to night time you may feel happy to let them sleep longer at night. This is totally down to you and the age of your baby as the recommended time to go without feeding at night between newborn and three months is no longer than three hours. Babies have small tummies and will need feeding often.

Go to chapter seven for more details or go to pages.abundant-baby.com to get a free taster of the Abundant Baby Sleep course and learn how to implement this method in your life for better sleep for the whole family.

28

Why is my baby waking up every 20 – 45 minutes?

Your baby is waking up every twenty - forty five minutes because they have entered a new phase of life where their sleep is more like an adult's sleep. This means unlike the newborn period, they're actually waking up in-between each phase of sleep. We *all* do this multiple times a night whether we are aware of it or not.

However, when a baby or toddler wakes up, they'll wake fully if their environment is different to the one they fell asleep in.

This is why (beyond three months) you can't feed a baby to sleep, rock or pat them. Unless you're in the exact same position, doing the exact same thing when your baby wakes up, they'll cry and search for you.

See chapter nine for more details or go to pages.abundant-baby.com to get a free taster of the Abundant Baby Sleep course and solve this sleep issue once and for all!

29

Why is my baby still not sleeping through the night?

If your baby is the right age to sleep through the night every night (nine months +) and they are ***not*** sleeping through the night, this is because you have taught them ***not*** to sleep through the night.

I know this is so frustrating to hear but by facing reality you can rectify what has happened and claim back your sleep.

So, first, analyse exactly what happens during the night. Are you feeding your baby? Talking to them loudly? Checking on them every time they make the tiniest of noises?

I know I was. With my first born, at the faintest mewl I was wide awake and wielding my boob about ready to feed her. I had laser hearing and thought the boob was the answer to everything.

This meant I had to wean my daughter off milk during the night and learn to listen outside the door (or on a baby monitor) instead of going in every time.

It quickly became clear that a cry I had previously thought was going to turn into a scream and would need immediate comfort, only actually lasted for a few seconds.

My baby was better off when I didn't go into her room because she was happy to roll over and go back to sleep. I wasn't being a bad mum by waiting outside the room and taking my time to come in. I was actually disturbing my baby less.

Read chapter twenty one to find out how to get your baby sleeping through the night from seven p.m. to seven a.m. or if you prefer video content go to pages.abundantbaby.com for a free mini taster of the Abundant Baby sleep course.

30

When is my baby physically able to sleep through the night?

When your baby can healthily sleep through the night is up for debate. Some sleep consultants say six months whereas others disagree. They say that not until twelve months of age will you see a consistent twelve hours of sleep every single night without fail.

I agree. Although you are probably like me and eager for a full night's sleep again, the truth is for the majority of the first year, your baby will need to be fed during the night and they will need you.

Being prepared to sacrifice some sleep for the first few months is a good idea as it gives you a realistic expectation. Depending on the baby, anything from ten months of age to be sleeping through the night is possible and healthy.

Sure, no one wants to hear they're gonna have to wait ten months or longer to have a full night's sleep but it's one of the many challenging (but totally worth it!) parts of being a parent.

It's one of the most tiring and tough parts for sure but it won't last.

In the meantime, by working on creating the right foundation for sleep you ensure your baby will sleep through the night as soon as they're ready.

The problem for parents is not a young baby refusing to sleep through the night but a baby of nine months or older or a toddler *still* not sleeping through the night! So by preparing excellent foundations now, you'll set yourself up for excellent sleep later.

Check out chapter six for the ideal wind down routine and chapter twenty one for a detailed explanation on how to get your baby sleeping through the night when they're ready.

Or go to pages.abundantbaby.com for a free taster of the Abundant Baby Sleep video course with worksheets, sleep schedules and lifetime access.

31

Why is my baby resisting sleep?

Your baby is resisting sleep for a variety of reasons. They could be overtired. This makes them release the stress hormone, cortisol, and makes them way more sad, stressed and in need of your help.

So, if your baby is stiffening up and screaming when you cuddle them, they're probably totally exhausted.

Stay as calm as you possibly can and try to soothe them and switch up the mood so the stressful situation changes and your baby can finally sleep.

Another possible reason: If your baby is three months or older they have now acquired object permanence. This means they can remember where they fell asleep, so if they wake up in a different place this will cause alarm and cause them to resist sleep.

Read chapter nine for more details or go to pages.abundantbaby.com to buy the extended Abundant Baby sleep video course where each sleep obstacle and stage of your baby's life is mapped out to ensure you both get excellent sleep forever.

32

What are sleep crutches?

Sleep crutches are the things your baby relies on to sleep that disrupt *your* sleep like a dummy/soother, feeding to sleep, rocking/patting or holding to sleep.

If your baby has gone to sleep breastfeeding or being patted on the back, when they wake up they'll immediately search for the exact situation they fell asleep in. Whether this is the hand that was patting them, the dummy, bottle or nipple they were sucking, or the arms that were cuddling them, they will wonder where they've gone and will cry to get them back.

This is why sleep crutches do not work as a long term way to get your baby to fall asleep. I know they work amazingly at the time but they don't work when your baby wakes up in the night, because you need sleep too!

Four common sleep crutches

- A dummy/soother
- Feeding to sleep
- Rocking/patting to sleep

- Holding to sleep

Go to chapter ten for a more detailed explanation or get a free taster of the Abundant Baby sleep course at pages.abundantbaby.com with effective ways of dealing with short naps, teething, separation anxiety, overstimulation and feeding at night.

33

What are sleep triggers?

Sleep triggers are the replacement for sleep crutches. A sleep trigger, like a sleep crutch is something that your baby becomes reliant on to go to sleep.

However, a sleep trigger is in your control. You have chosen it and so it aids your sleep rather than disrupts it.

Sleep triggers

- A sleeping bag
- Lullaby music (Try the Brian Eno Apollo album)
- Darkness
- Sucking their thumb

Go to chapter ten to read more or get a free taster of the Abundant Baby sleep course at pages.abundantbaby.com for age appropriate modules and solutions to sleep barriers like teething, separation anxiety and short naps.

34

How often should my baby be napping at 3 months?

At three months your baby should be napping as and when they want. The total sleep needed for a three - four month baby is **14.5 hours.**

During the day: 3.5 - 4 hours

At night: 10 - 11 hours

While timings are helpful, at this stage the most important thing is to observe your baby.

All babies are different so while they'll need similar amounts of sleep, it won't be exactly the same. Sleep signals govern whether you put your baby down for a nap at this stage, not example sleep schedules.

Go to chapter nine to find out what sleep signals are and begin an excellent nap experience for both you and your baby.

Or go to pages.abundantbaby.com for a free taster of the Abundant Baby Sleep programme with video tutorials and a detailed breakdown of sleep obstacles like teething, early morning wakings and short naps.

35

When can I start a sleep routine?

You can begin a sleep routine for your baby as early as three months old.

At this young age your baby will not always stick to a routine but it can be useful to have a loose one to follow. The sleep routine will form naturally around when your baby is tired.

By watching out for sleep signals, you'll know exactly when your baby is tired and be able to give them a nap as soon as possible. This ensures your baby gets plenty of sleep in the day which will promote sleep at night time too!

Read chapter nine for more details about sleep signals and nap times.

You could also go to chapter seven to read about the things you can do before your baby is old enough for a sleep routine. These important additions will set excellent habits in place, making sleep easier for both you and your baby.

If you prefer in-depth video tutorials go to pages.abundant-baby.com to get a free taster of the full extended Abundant Baby Sleep course.

36

How many hours of sleep should a newborn get?

There is no rule when it comes to sleep for a newborn baby. They should sleep as often and as long as they want. This rules applies to night *and* day.

Your newborn baby needs as much as seventeen hours of sleep. You heard me right, seventeen hours! That's why it can often feel like all your baby does is sleep.

This sleep will loosely consist of seven - nine hours at night and eight hours during the day but it does not need to be monitored.

Basically, relax as much as you can. Know that your baby is getting all the sleep they need in order to grow and develop.

If you're eager to get started with a sleep routine, there are a few gentle and important things you can introduce to your baby at this early stage, which will help you to lay down the foundation for excellent sleep.

Read chapter eight for more details or go to pages.abundant-baby.com for a free taster of the full Abundant Baby video sleep course.

37

How do I put my baby down to sleep drowsy but awake?

This is THE question. Isn't drowsy but awake the most frustrating phrase in the world?!

I lost count of the amount of blog posts I read in the early stages of my daughter's life which said, 'Put your baby down drowsy but awake'.

I remember thinking, well if I could do that, there wouldn't be a problem!

I couldn't find a simple explanation of what drowsy but awake actually *meant*, never mind how on earth I would make it happen.

So, here it is: A simple definition without any further delay.

Drowsy but awake means ready for sleep but not asleep yet.

In the first few months of your baby's life this is a nearly impossible state to create because your baby will fall asleep instantly. It's a fine line for sure between asleep and awake so don't worry too much about it.

I found that after three months (which is when the phrase will begin to apply to you) it made more sense. My baby was nearly asleep but not quite.

If my baby was feeding there was still some suction (it had slowed but it was still there) and when I put them down to sleep they would stir slightly.

This is the best way to achieve drowsy but awake at this early stage.

As your baby gets slightly older, four or five months old, you will actually be putting them down in their cot when they're obviously awake.

This is when the phrase becomes easier to understand because the line between awake and asleep is not as blurred.

All you have to do, is observe your baby closely and watch for their sleep signs. By taking them up to nap when they display the sleep signs, you'll be putting them down in their cot to process their day before they fall asleep. They'll be drowsy but awake!

Go to chapters nine and ten to understand sleep signs and sleep windows in more detail. If you prefer video content go to pages.abundantbaby.com for a free taster of the full extended Abundant Baby sleep course.

38

How do I avoid crying at sleep times?

Crying at sleep times is so upsetting and often feels like there is no possible way this will ever be avoided. It's the worst thing ever because all you want is your baby to be happy.

Why does sleep have to be a stressful time?

Here's the reason why: Your baby has learned sleep habits that suit neither you or them.

You may not even be aware that you have created sleep habits but by slowing down and working out exactly what is happening at nap and bedtimes you will recognise the routine you have unknowingly created.

You'll be able to implement a whole new set of habits that will, in a few weeks (or a few days for some babies), lead to absolutely no crying at nap and bed time.

Read chapter six for the perfect wind down routine or go to pages.abundantbaby.com to get a free taster of the Abundant Baby sleep video course including in-depth solutions to overcome sleep obstacles at every age.

39

Will I ever sleep again?!

I know how you feel!! This was my question and no one had the answer!

The actual answer is annoyingly vague.

It is different for every baby and parent because it depends on the age and temperament of your baby.

However, a more satisfying and specific one size fits all answer is: It is possible to achieve a full night's sleep between ten and twelve months.

This can feel like a long time to wait but by this age it will not be a one off, you will get twelve hours of sleep every night forever.

Of course, there are things that can disturb your sleep as your baby gets older like colds and teething, but they're easier to deal with when you have banked months of wonderful sleep and can rely on a solid foundation of excellent sleep habits.

If your baby is already past twelve months then the answer is: You'll get a full night's sleep in two - four weeks.

All you have to do is remove the current sleep habits you have created, whether knowingly or unknowingly, and replace them with the Abundant Baby ideal wind down routine in chapter six.

If you have time, read this whole book and get the Abundant Baby sleep course at abundantbaby.com/sleep to understand each age bracket in detail and be prepared for every milestone and new development.

This way you'll be ready for whatever comes your way and you'll have a water-tight sleep routine for the whole family.

X

Goodbye and Good Luck!

Thank you for being with me during this book.

If you're not ready to say goodbye and would like a free taster of the full extended Abundant Baby Sleep video course go to pages.abundantbaby.com

Module by module, you will learn how to go from zero hours of sleep to twelve hours of sleep every night for the rest of your baby's life.

You'll start looking forward to nap and bedtimes and sleep will no longer be something you dread. The video course is the perfect accompaniment to this book.

40

The Extended Abundant Baby Sleep Video Course

Do you need help with . . .?

- Stopping the early morning wakings - no more 5 a.m starts!
- Lengthening short day naps
- Understanding why your baby resists sleep
- Teething, separation anxiety and common colds
- Embracing major milestones - how to cope with crawling and standing in the cot
- Understanding sleep schedules at each stage

The Abundant Baby Sleep course is for you.

You can enjoy:

- Lifetime access
- Constantly updated modules
- Years worth of research and experience packed into one

course of six modules that grow with your baby from newborn to 4 years and beyond

- Sleep schedules designed to give your baby the rest and rejuvenation they need to get the most out of each day, avoid tantrums and learn at a healthy pace
- Ways to overcome sleep regressions, short naps, colds, nightmares, separation anxiety, teething and constant night awakenings
- A video version of the ideal wind down routine in chapter six of this book
- Simplified versions of each chapter in this book with video content and worksheets
- 24/7 access which fits around your life and is always there for you to drop into whether you're in your PJs, work clothes or covered in baby milk!

About the Author

I'm Tilly and I have two little girls (princesses, unicorns and scooters galore in our house) who are 2 and 4.

I first became interested in sleep when I stopped getting any!! When Millie (my first born) reached nine months I was exhausted. I couldn't go on. I knew something had to change. She was waking up every 45 minutes for milk.

After two months of research and tears (mainly from me!) Millie began sleeping 12 hours every night and has done ever since.

When my second daughter was born everything was easy because I had my sleep plan at the ready. She was sleeping through the night at 11 months.

I don't actually recommend a full stretch of 12 hours before the age of 11 months. Some babies can do 12 hours at 9 months but most would rather not.

6 - 8 hours is totally doable though and something you can learn to rely on from 6 months or earlier when you follow my sleep rules and lay the right foundation down.

Last year, my sleep clients and friends finally convinced me to put all my sleep lessons and research into the Abundant Baby Sleep Course! I'm so proud of it and hope it helps you at a time when you need it the most. Trust me, I've been there!

You can connect with me on:

https://www.abundantbaby.com

Subscribe to my newsletter:

https://pages.abundantbaby.com

Printed in Great Britain
by Amazon

42372865R00106